IGNITING THE INVISIBLE TRIBE

Designing An Organization That Doesn't Suck

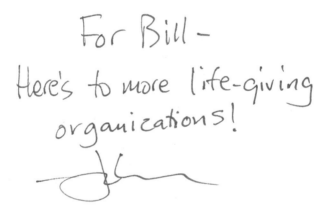

For Bill –
Here's to more life-giving
organizations!

Josh Allan Dykstra

PRAISE

"Josh has a great way of talking with you, not writing at you. You feel he's here with you, with brandy in both your hands, next to a roaring fire. The resulting conversation is one that will change your view on business and life. Tribes are better for Josh's work."

— Dave Logan, Ph.D.

New York Times #1 bestselling coauthor of *Tribal Leadership* & *The Three Laws of Performance*

"This book gets your attention; no, demands it. With unsettling observations, challenging questions, and even more compelling options, you get to let your mind soar on the wings of dreams about meaningful work. Don't just buy this book; devour it, and use it to help invent the future we'd love to work in."

— Terry Paulson, Ph.D.

Award-winning speaker and author of *The Optimism Advantage, They Shoot Managers Don't They,* and *Leadership Truths One Story at a Time*

"The rules of organizational life have changed dramatically and Josh provides a new and reliable map of the territory. Prepare to change. His strategies for thriving—not just surviving—will illuminate the path forward for all of us!"

— Michael W. Morrison, Ph.D.

Founder of the University of Toyota and author of *The Other Side of the Card*

"Igniting the Invisible Tribe is a call to recognize the terrific advantages of 'what will be' in the emerging 21st century workplace. Josh's well-honed perspective turns traditional workforce planning on its ear while clearly offering new ways to collaboratively reach a better tomorrow. The book is forcefully explicit, an easy but provocative reading experience and loaded with ideas all generations in the workforce should hear."

— Carleen MacKay

Director of Mature Workforce Initiatives for Career Partners International and author or co-author of 4 books about and for the Boomer Workforce

CONTENTS

NEW RULES

NEW TOOLS

This book is a manifesto for a new kind of business.

I don't know your story, but I suspect that your life, like mine, is incredibly imbalanced. If you are like me, we spend the vast majority of our time and energy on one thing:

Work.

I spend more time working than I spend on anything else.

Work occupies me more than my family, more than my hobbies, more than relaxing. It absorbs most of my thoughts and the vast majority of my energy.

Isn't it only right, then, that my "place of business" not suck?

This section is about discovering new answers to some very old questions.

W*hat was I going to do?*

I had been fired before, but this time was different.

The time of the First Firing, I had been in college. I was the Student Director for the largest and most visible program at the school. The "adult" Director and I never saw eye-to-eye, and after a tumultuous year and a half of working together, when I returned from my study abroad semester at the end of my junior year, he had moved on. He then calmly informed me that I would be moving on, too.

I wasn't so calm, then.

The Second Firing was better. This time it was almost mutual, even.

But that didn't help me know what to do.

Last time, I was a kid. Nineteen years old. This time I was in my late twenties. I had a wife. I wanted to start a family soon. Wasn't I supposed to have *something* figured out by now?

Well, I didn't have a clue.

It was the end of 2008. My job in the sprawling, high desert suburb of Los Angeles had ended and the economy was taking a deep dive into the proverbial crapper. I had just entered grad school to get an MBA focused in Executive Leadership, though I didn't fully grasp what that meant. (Getting a degree is like a kid trying to catch a squirrel—it seems like a good idea, but we're never quite sure what we'll do once we have it.) A small consulting firm near Pasadena had brought me on as an intern the past spring, and now they agreed to hire me in a more part-time capacity.

At least I knew *that* much.

In my social circles, people were kind. They told me that successful people get fired fairly often. Apparently I was on my way.

Some people know exactly what they want to do with their life. Others, notsomuch. By the time of the Second Firing, I had perfected the art of the meandering career path. I had worked in small cafes, enormous Fortune 50 organizations, retail stores, tiny offices, restaurants, government agencies, a construction company, a university, a radio station, and a nonprofit. I had done mind-numbing data entry, managed a team of 50+ people, made pizzas, and brewed coffee. I had created and ran an intern program, been an on-air disc jockey, ripped shingles off rooftops, recorded albums and performed my own music in front of thousands of people. I had written proposals and managed budgets. I had coached executives and executed new business programs. I had done a whole lot of stuff, but there didn't seem to be much of a common thread.

At the time of the First Firing, I was swimming in possibilities. This time, I had been out of college for more than half a decade and was toiling away in what university students longingly call "the real world."

Sadly, the "real" world felt pretty *fake* to me.

My head was filled with memories of, almost exclusively, *school*, which prepared me for... what, exactly? A meaningless job? An endless climb up the "corporate ladder?" Or maybe a life of purpose... with a nice side dish of "eternal struggle to pay the rent?"

Something wasn't connecting.

Even more strangely, many people around me seemed to feel the same way I did, but being an "adult" seemed to come with an invisible instruction manual containing one rule:

IGNORE THE DISCONNECT.

"Ignore that you spend the majority of your time—the only resource you never get back—in a job you don't like, being treated like a machine, doing things that kind of ruin the planet."

And, suddenly, there it was.

The common thread.

All through my winding journey, they had been there: the miserable people who hated their jobs. They were at each of my stops. Sometimes I filled the role myself, and sometimes it was another unlucky sucker. But tragically, unhappiness at work was *always* present.

A vision had entered my mind. Perhaps *this* was my calling—**to help end workplace misery**.

Have you ever known one of these miserable work people?

Have you ever been one?

Chances are good that you can answer YES to *both* of those questions.

What if we could go to work and love what we do *every day?* What if we could have jobs that used our unique abilities and talents? What if our work wasn't just time spent in exchange for a paycheck, but was in service of something profoundly meaningful to us? What if we actually made a difference—a real impact on the world—with our jobs?

It seems noble, but... *really?*

I imagine my utopian tone sounds rather trite. Most likely, you are a person who earned good grades in school (and even if this isn't the case, it wasn't because you *couldn't*). You probably worked hard to get to where you are. If you're in a career, you've paid more than your share of dues. Your own path has taught you to make peace with the way the world "is."

You prefer to call it "reality," not cynicism or being jaded.

But think about your kids (even if they don't exist yet). Then think about *their* kids. And maybe *their* kids. Don't you want something just a little better for *them?*

This section is called "New Answers," not "New Questions," because we've certainly pondered these questions before. But something special is happening right now. For potentially the first time in human history, we have a convergence of things happening which give us **new answers**.

Is the "real world"—as it is now—*really* the best we can do?

No, it's not.

IS
WORK
SUPPOSED TO
SUCK?

When it comes to our work, we often can't connect the dots. We can't join heart and head. We have a bunch of emotional baggage that keeps nagging us from the inside, insisting that work should, well... *feel like work*.

To this I have one question:

Who says?

Who says work needs to feel hard or be painful? *Who says* work should be unfulfilling or tedious? *Who says* work must simultaneously take more of our time and be more miserable than anything else in our lives? *Who says* work has to feel like "work"?

Who says work has to suck?

More importantly, *why have we accepted this as true?*

Over the thousands of years humans have roamed

the planet, we've found many ways to work. From our days as hunters and gatherers to the complex multinational corporate behemoths of the 21st Century, the way we "do business" with each other has continually evolved, sometimes in strange and unexpected ways. But the reality is that for almost all of us, our work occupies the great majority of our lives. We begin working in some capacity when we are teenagers and never really stop. It doesn't matter if we are a tour guide in Beijing, an owner of a children's bookstore in Prague, or a steel worker in Ohio, whatever we do for work defines what the rest of our life can look like. And strangely, despite the fact that the vast majority of our existence is taken with this singular topic of **work**, we spend almost no time thinking about *why* we work the way we do.

The fact that we don't often think about our motivations for work is an important insight in itself. Realizing this disconnect helps us answer the chapter title's question—*Is work supposed to suck?*— because it turns out the answer is NO. It *isn't* supposed to. We're just so busy that we don't have the time or space to internalize that reality.

The other challenge about work is that, like parenting, it's not taught, it's *caught*. This largely explains why we work the way we do (and why it's so hard to change): we see the way our parents work, or our teachers work, or our first managers work, and *we just do that*. It's habit. We don't think about why, we don't stop to ponder, we don't question anything, really; we just *get to work*. We "catch" whatever work styles our role models display just like we catch a virus.

The outcome is that, unless we are blessed with excellent examples (quite rare) or are able to educate ourselves about healthy, life-giving ways to work (hard to find time to do this with all the "work" we have to do!), we're pretty much stuck doing whatever our role models did. It's not intentional bad practice, it's just ignorance.[1] The sad result is that we end up feeling like work IS supposed to suck, because the sucky kind is all we've ever seen modeled.

Then, on top of all these personal misunderstandings about the point of work, we've got organizational structures that *make it worse*.

Think about all the monumental innovations that have occurred in most areas of business, from technology to operations to sales to finance. Despite these advances, there have been virtually *no* real-world changes in the area of organizational design. We could be part of a brilliant new startup building the most progressive, cutting-edge products on the planet, but when it comes to systemizing the way we work together in an organization, we default back to a "departmental model" that hasn't changed in decades (and is really just a continuation of "scientific management," which started over 100 years ago!).

This seems ridiculous (and pretty much is), but there are a few good reasons for it.

First, org charts aren't very sexy. There are many things we can work with that have a "sexy factor" (designer shoes, iPhones, shiny new cars), but the "structure of our company" definitely doesn't go in that category.

Second, organizational structures are an invisible, conceptual thing. We can't hold them in our hands or capture them in a photograph or put a soundtrack to them. This makes working with them inherently more challenging.

Third, as we've already talked about, we are socially conditioned not to think about WHY we work the way we do. It's been clearly communicated to us that "work" means *doing a task,* and anything that doesn't fit snugly in that bucket is clearly "not work."

But we can no longer underestimate the power of these invisible structures we work in, because they create the boundaries we work within. They are the rules. And rules are very, *very* important.

Probably even more important than we realize.

Think of a sports game—what determines how the players play? The rules. What determines the actions they perform on the field/court? The rules. What determines how they spend their time, both during the game and between matches? The rules. What determines what they get paid for, and how much money they make? The rules.

In business, our organizational structures are the

rules. They are the "guidelines on the field," the social agreements which give us the boundaries for how we can interact with each other. Our structures tell us what we're allowed to do at work. And while it's evident that the external rules of business (how we compete due to technology, globalization, etc.) have changed **dramatically** in the last few decades, *the **internal** rules which govern our work relationships have not.*

Unless we can change our organizations at this structural level, the disconnect will create some serious problems for where work is headed.

In fact, we're already feeling the destructive effects.

IGNITION POINT

How can we use these ideas to begin transforming the way we work? Answer the following questions to start a fire of your own:

If money were no object, what would I want out of life? What would I do with my time?

Deep down, do I truly believe work can be life-giving? What does life-giving work look like to me?

(Think about the greatest leader you've personally known.) In my eyes, what are a few qualities that made this leader so great?

How can I treat people more like the greatest leader I've known does/did?

WHO CREATES THE FUTURE?

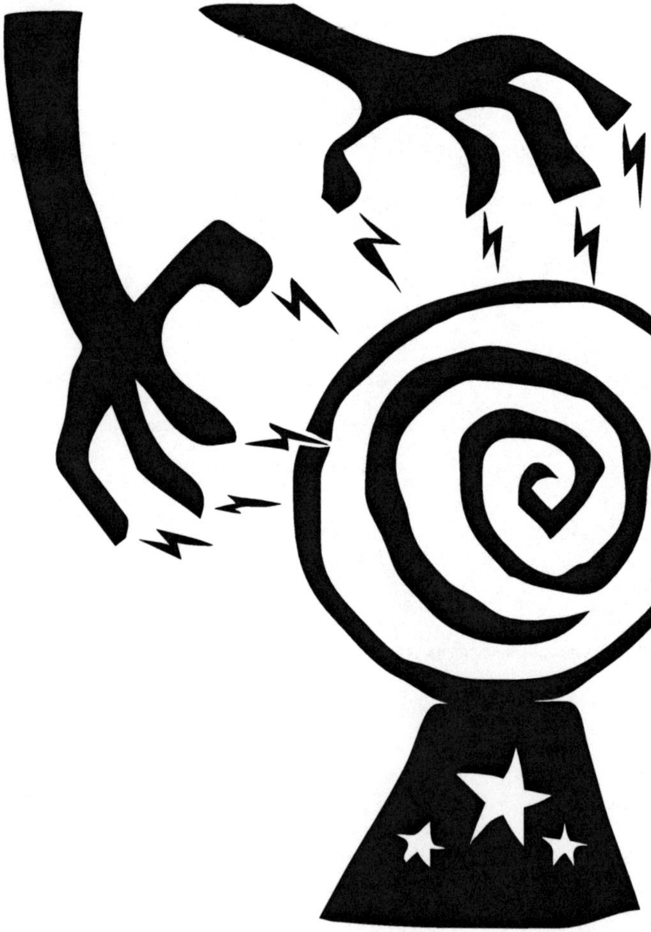

When we think about the future, many of us see more of this:

Chaos.

In business, we certainly find chaos everywhere these days.

Not only are people losing their jobs, they're losing their retirement and their sense of stability. The large corporation, yesterday's bulwark of job security, doesn't provide "loyalty" as a perk of employment any longer. New technologies replace tasks people used to do. College grads exit universities with passionate plans to change the world and instead of a job, find themselves back in their parents' basements. Even fields like doctoring and lawyering, specialties adults used to pray for their child to choose, don't carry the guarantee they used to.

The tectonic shift in today's workplace is taking prisoners from everything. Nothing is safe.

Every year as I travel, speak, write, and consult, I talk with hundreds of wonderful people. And the pattern of these conversations is remarkably similar. Once we get past formalities, sometimes after a few drinks, an unsettling sentiment gets unearthed. In their slightly more vulnerable moments, they share that when it comes to work they feel like the ground is eroding from under their feet, like sand rushing back to the depths as the ocean recedes.

No one seems to know *why* or *how* the world is changing exactly, only that it most certainly is.

The next part of the dialogue is equally predictable. Because they don't know *why* or *how* things are changing, fear paralyzes the conversation from going any further. Defense mechanisms kick in and a joke is made, or the subject is stealthily changed. It's far easier to bury the problem. Ignore it. We're all in the same boat, right? Like they say: prediction is extremely difficult—especially about the future. *Nobody* knows what's coming.

This would be fine, except *the future doesn't work like that.*

We have this notion that "the future" is a specific destination point, the big red ending dot on some kind of metaphysical map.

But this isn't true.

The future is just the culmination of the millions of tiny decisions we—all of us humans—are collectively making *right now*, at this very instant, all across the world. By reading this book, you are *changing the future.* How? By spending your time here instead of doing something else somewhere else.

The future isn't a static destination we will someday "arrive at." It is a continually evolving entity, shaped like clay by billions of pairs of human hands, all across the globe, all the time.

To a very real extent, *we make the future whatever it will be by what we do now.*[2]

This is why it's so important that we find a way to finish the scary discussion started above. It is with these conversations that we are literally creating the future of the world.

So why shouldn't we create a better one?

Research firms like The Gallup Organization and Towers Watson find regularly that somewhere around two-thirds of Americans are not engaged in their jobs. A 2011 report from Deloitte found that **79%** of people employed by a company are not passionate about what they do. [3]

This is a *catastrophic* waste. It is a waste of human time and talent, and it is a waste of energy that could be used productively in our organizations. [4]

And we *know it*.

Companies spend a huge amount of money on personal development and individual training trying to fix this problem. But much of it never changes anything, at least not in a major way—if it did, we'd see more movement in the above statistics.

Is it possible that the solution isn't in the *training*, but in how we've structured the *tribe?*

For far too long, we've organized ourselves in archaic, destructive ways. We know better, but the lure of the old world has been too strong.

No longer.

Now, the global climate is ripe for change. The spirit of revolution is in the air. The effects of business globalization, new technologies, emerging generations, the proliferation of democracy, and a striking new mentality about what human beings want from their work-lives is about to change the entire world.

In fact, it's already happening.

Our conversations are shifting. Our nouns and verbs are becoming words like *cooperation, collaboration,* and *creativity.* We are starting to talk in terms of *transparency, openness,* and *wellbeing.* We speak of *B-corporations* and *social enterprises.*

I'm guessing you've noticed this, too. (Language is a **big** deal; we'll revisit this idea later.)

As the story changes, so do the behaviors. The future is being rewritten before our eyes, and this future is all about *how everything connects.*

CAN
BUSINESS
SAVE THE
WORLD?

W e used to think we could just "punch the clock" at the office in order to make the money we needed to live our "real life" outside of work. We thought when we went home, we left our work at the office.

This was an illusion.

We now know that human beings *can't* compartmentalize in this way, and that a person's career has more impact on their general wellbeing than perhaps anything else.[5]

There is *no* separation of work from life. Even when we try our best to keep them apart, a stressful day instantly brings them crashing back together as we take out work frustrations on our family members.

Besides, where do you spend most of your waking hours? If you're anything like me, the answer to that is easy: *"At work."*

If we're going to improve the quality of our lives, *the most direct path is to improve the way we work.*

But that's not all.

Business is now the most powerful force on the planet.[6] Multinational corporations with more cash than the nations they span are now the norm, but the economic, environmental, and emotional impact of our current businesses are unsustainable on the good end of the spectrum and flat-out evil at the worst.

If we're going to make the world a better place to live, *the most direct path is to improve the way we work.*

SO...

*If we are going to solve the **individual wellbeing problem,** we have to fix business.*

*To solve the **world's challenges,** we have to fix business.*

Whether we're talking about your life or about the future of the globe, saving the world is all about changing the way we work.

We *need* a work revolution.

This incredulous disconnect between "job" and "purpose" *isn't* the best we can do.

If we can get work right, it could be one of the *best* parts of our lives.

Instead of what makes life suck, it could be the very thing that makes it *great*.

The world is indeed changing in fundamental ways, and though many people see chaos and storms on the horizon, what's actually coming is something else:

HOPE.

The ways in which the world is changing are the very things that can show us a new way to work and a better way to live. The work revolution has already begun, and it will *help us* create businesses that are fulfilling and meaningful.

IGNITION POINT

How can we use these ideas to begin transforming the way we work? Answer the following questions to start a fire of your own:

Do I really believe I can help create the future? Why or why not?

What are a few "interesting" (new, strange, unfamiliar) words becoming part of the conversations around me?

What was the last "spillover" (positive or negative) of work into my home life? How did it affect my overall wellbeing?

Instead of trying to find a mythical "balance" between work and life, how can I focus on creating work that gives me energy instead of being draining?

NEW
WORLD

Even if we don't often admit it, most of us have occasional moments of transcendent clarity. We experience moments when the clouds part in our mind, a light shines through, and suddenly the world seems peaceful. It's like we can see things as they truly are, if only for a second. In those rare instances, we can *feel* in the air that the world is changed, somehow. We sense *something* is different.

The challenge is we're not really sure *what the heck happened*. The differences seem too widespread, too global, too varied—just too massive—to wrap our minds around.

This is a problem, though, because understanding what has changed is an essential part of the story if we wish to know *how to respond*.

In this section we'll bring these big, unwieldy changes down to earth. We'll explore them in everyday language, and begin connecting the dots.

We'll start to see the new world as it is.

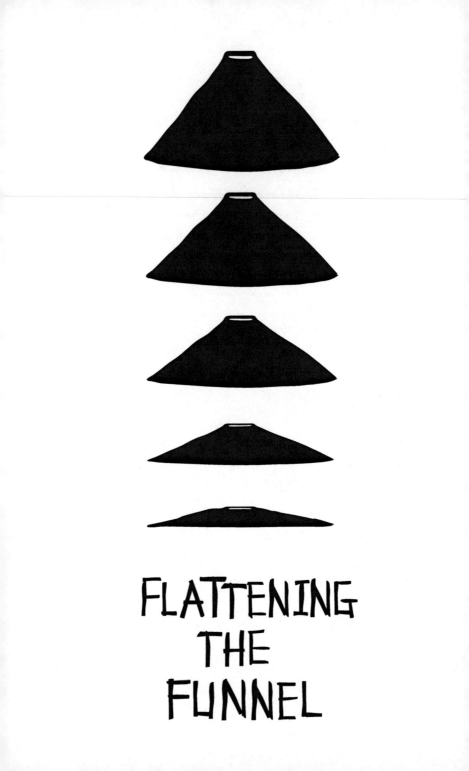

FLATTENING
THE
FUNNEL

Our global society has changed in fundamental, tectonic ways over the past few decades, and much of it has to do with how we communicate with each other.

Until very recently, humanity had one real tool to communicate—something I call the "upside-down funnel." The few at the "top," who throughout history have been priests, kings, or wealthy people (sometimes all three at once), would perch atop the funnel and speak "down" to the masses.

Not anymore.

This power structure has been completely flattened. Now, communication is more like an endless field of humans, with each person holding a megaphone and talking to (or yelling at) anyone who will listen.

Much has been discussed about how this shift

is changing the way we broadcast, but I'm more interested in how it affects the way we *listen*.

This perspective sparks a peculiar question:

"When we can listen to anyone, who do we listen to?"

In all of human history, this has never, *ever*, been a relevant question. But suddenly it is. We're now being forced to make choices in response to inquiries no humans on the planet have ever had to ponder before.

Who *do* we listen to if we can listen to anyone?[7]

The answer might be simpler than we expect.

We listen to the people who are most interesting. We talk about the things that are most remark-able. And we give our attention to whatever we are most passionate about in that particular moment.

We filter. We choose. And we pick the things that naturally give us energy.

We really have no other option. Humans simply weren't built for the kind of information overload we're currently experiencing.

We can now listen to virtually anyone on the planet, with each person claiming his or her unique worldview, opinion, and soapbox. But the rest of us human beings do not have the capacity, or interest, to hear it *all*. So, with the option to listen to anyone, we make *choices* about where to shift our attention. And when we make these choices, which are usually unconscious, we naturally place ourselves into groups of people who like what we do. We find our way into communities that share our passions and interests.

We are naturally filtering ourselves into *invisible tribes*.

The internet, particularly in its current "social" form, hasn't been around very long, but we already know a little about how it's reshaping culture. For example, we know that in all likelihood, no matter the esoteric or bizarre nature of our interests, there are other people "out there" who like what we do. If you happen to be a fan of a comic book from the 1970's about mutant dolphins, a man who wants to know how to better care for his long hair, or a huge fan of chewing ice, there is a place for you online. (I only made up one of those.)[8] We know there are millions of niche groups on almost any conceivable topic.[9]

This is wonderful for camaraderie, fun, and expanding our minds, but... is that is the extent of it?

Are strange niche communities (and cat videos) the only things the internet is good for?

I don't think so.

Explore this with me for a moment.

We understand there are tribes for everything, online. We understand some tribes are small and others are gargantuan. We also recognize that each tribe has *something* which draws them together, and that on the internet the things that have divided human beings since the beginning of time—things like nationality, gender, orientation, geography, and even language— often melt away. Online we have the ability to project the "me" that we want most to be, and this opportunity allows us to connect with people we'd never be able (or willing) to connect with otherwise.

Right now, most people in these growing tribes *don't know the others in the tribe exist*. Many think they are alone in their passions. New social technologies are connecting them... but they don't realize it yet.

This is why they are an *invisible* tribe.

At this transitional time, these groups are mostly invisible to each other and to the world at large. Fifty years ago we might go most, if not all, of our lives without meeting the other people who shared our particular (or peculiar) interests. This is getting increasingly hard to do. Our technologies are "pushing" us all closer together.

We know these tribes exist, but what do they have to do with business?

What if leaders and entrepreneurs were able to take these invisible tribes and give them a great place to work on what they are most passionate about?

What if we were to find a group of people *already excited* about something—we know they're out there—and provide them a new kind of container/structure/architecture in which to meet each other and connect and brainstorm and accomplish great stuff together?

What if leaders could harness the collective discretionary energy of a group by liberating them to focus it in a direction they *already care about?*[10]

There is certainly opportunity online for small niche groups, but we don't have to be limited in this way. There are also much larger groups that are interested in convening action around things like environmental issues, parenting, and health care.[11] There are invisible tribes obsessed with sustainable food growth, progressive education, better communication, and on and on.

Do each of these groups need a leader? *Yes.*

Could that leader be you? *Hell yes.*

But is this enough?

No.

Many authors and thought leaders explore the idea of becoming a "tribe leader" in great detail. Make no mistake—this is crucial.

But it's only one side of the coin.

THE OTHER SIDE OF THE COIN

The way humans think about work is evolving.

We want *more* than we did before. We are no longer willing to exchange meaningless, empty labor for a paycheck. For most of us, it used to be worth the trade—mostly because we had no choice.

It's not anymore. We have options we've never had before.

Unfortunately, even though our mindset is changing, most of our business systems aren't.

Our businesses suck.

While this is certainly great fun to say, I mean it in the most literal way possible. Our companies—how they are structured now—suck literally in (at least) three ways:

1) They suck the resources from our planet—often with no long-term thought of repercussions;

2) They suck the life out of us, the people who work for them, by treating us like we are machines; and

3) They suck the meaning from existence, through pointless tasks that don't create any authentic value for us or for larger society.

Oftentimes, they also suck in the more "informal" sense by being too slow, too bureaucratic, and too static.

The organizational systems we've built encourage slowness over speed and command and control over collaboration.

They emphasize process over passion and homogeneousness over imagination.

They reward rule-makers instead of rule-breakers.

But a slow, process-driven, rule-filled world isn't the world we live in.

At least, not anymore.

Our companies are built for a different time, playing by yesterday's rules, not tomorrow's.

They're living in a world that doesn't exist.

This is a bit scary, if we stop and think about it. Our business models—the very things that provide our livelihoods, pay our rent, and buy food for our kids— are built on *terribly* antiquated practices. In most of our companies, we are using the organizational equivalents of lobotomies and bloodletting to try to fix our problems. These destructive, outdated practices aren't making anything better—and in many cases make things worse.

Let me provide a few examples.

PHONE TREES

Would someone like to stand up and explain how an endless phone tree system helps customers feel "their call is important?"[12] The only thing these modern-day torture devices do, when we finally break through to a representative, is condition us to forget that the person on the other end is a real human being.

PERFORMANCE REVIEWS

Can anyone actually make the argument that a typical weakness-focused performance review helps a business work better?[13] Is helping us suck a little less than we did last year *really* our best path to excellence?[14]

POWERPOINTS

How many people would willingly volunteer to sit through a mile-long list of bullet points and a droning presentation? Are we to believe this is the best possible way to communicate important information?[15]

Do any of these things create any kind of *real* value? No, they are simply relics of a bygone era (and it would be nice if they'd all go away *faster*).

It's clear that we need to improve many things about the way we work, but to do this we must see *both* sides of the coin. Individual leadership is vital, but it's not the only force at work.

Our organizations all contain a mix of these two invisible dynamics:

First, there's an invisible "me."[16]

Each of us, individually, has an invisible world of our own. We have our own mindset and perspective— our paradigm, how we see reality. This internal lens constantly shapes our worldview and manifests itself out into the physical realm, shaping the reality we perceive around us.

I often think that life really is like a stage, perhaps in a slightly different way than William Shakespeare envisioned. When we see a musical or production of a play, we recognize that what happens on the stage is dictated to a large degree by what goes on *backstage*.

Additional cast are waiting in the wings. Sets for the next scene are hiding out of sight. Sound amplification and lighting canisters are concealed. All are powerful contributors to communicating the story, but we see *none* of them directly.

The way we act in our daily lives is almost entirely determined by what's going on "backstage" in our minds.[17] We all have opinions, paradigms, and perspectives. These things form our worldview. Our worldview, in turn, forms the world around us.

This is the first side of the coin. Most self-help books, seminars, coaches, and organizational initiatives focus on this side.

It's very important. It's just not the whole picture.

Second, there's an invisible "we."[18]

This is the "tribe" part—the other side of the coin. Whenever a group of people come together a unique culture is formed, and this sense of togetherness becomes a power unto itself.

Individuals in the group—typically the leaders—impart rules that govern the way the group acts, but over time these policies take on a life of their own. The culture of a tribe is a direct outgrowth of these systemized routines.

Before long, the invisible rules begin to dictate back to the members how they are supposed to behave. Without a leader's deliberate care or careful architecting, these unseen forces begin telling *us* how we are to behave.

There's a phrase used in consulting circles that says "Culture eats strategy for breakfast." This statement describes the invisible force every organizational leader must contend with if he or she wishes to change *anything*. The invisible juggernaut of "culture" is like a gale force wind, and it will blow through any idea, strategy, or program that doesn't get deeply rooted.

In our businesses, this "group" side of work—the *tribe* side of the coin—is mostly ignored. Though we talk about collaboration a lot, we rarely see changes that help groups *work better*. If not missing altogether, a focus on the tribe usually gets stuck looking like feeble "team building" exercises that don't ever seem to create more efficient or energized relationships, at least not in a large way.

Right now, we focus almost all of our organizational change efforts on the single person. We send leaders to training sessions to learn about their *individual* deficiencies. We purchase *personal* coaching for our high potentials. We buy our managers *self*-help books. While this can be great and helpful, it's all about "me," not "we."

It's only one side of what we need.

All of the personal development in the world can't fix a problem that lives in the *system*. It's like treating cancer with a band-aid.

We must fix the way the organization is organized.[19] We must build better human systems. We must address the *structure*.[20]

It's *not* enough to be willing to lead a tribe. We also need to know HOW to lead them. We must learn how to build new social structures that align with the imagination and passion these tribes possess. We will fail if we attempt to lead them into a brave new world with expired old methods.

When we begin to see the world differently, we can glimpse the "new rules" for the "new game."

We can find ways to ignite the tribes all around us.

IGNITING
THE
INVISIBLE
TRIBE

Many years of human evolution have taught us that we can accomplish far more together than we can apart.

For all the individualized power of the new economy, people have forever grouped into tribes to work, and we always will. Furthermore, the emerging economy is built on a foundation of interconnectedness. Because of this, those who will be successful in the world of tomorrow will be the individuals and organizations that find a way to *capitalize on these connections.*

At this very moment, there are a number of significant shifts all happening at once, from remarkable technology innovations, to the continuing globalization of business, to a collective shift in consciousness, to hyper-connected emerging generations.[21] This convergence is refashioning the world into a collaborative, connected web of relationships and information, and as we've discussed, the overwhelming nature of it all is "pushing" us into self-filtered groups called invisible tribes.

If leaders or entrepreneurs wish to accomplish something great in a world filled with invisible tribes, there are two immediate concerns:

1) "How do we find these groups?" and

2) "How do we help them do great work?"

It used to be almost impossible to find and organize an invisible tribe. There was simply no practical way to execute it; we were limited by our geographies, physical relationships, and economic resources. But now, anyone with an internet connection or an iPhone renders these barriers irrelevant.

In all likelihood, the tribe you're looking for is *already connected*, and becoming more so with every minute that passes.

The world is doing the finding for us.

A marketplace full of invisible tribes feels unfamiliar,

but it comes with some incredible benefits. As one example (we'll continue to discuss more advantages throughout this book), it makes recruiting and hiring much easier. In yesterday's system, *"How do we get people to work for our company?"* is a popular and necessary question, and companies spend **big** bucks trying to answer it.

In the new world, however, this question is on the wrong side of the "upside-down funnel." Instead of trying to talk to *everyone,* we can now just reach into our already existing networks to connect with the larger tribe. We simply find the people who are **already passionate** about our particular endeavor or cause and we make them visible to their larger tribe. (Hopefully, many tribe members will already be working with us!) No longer do we have to interrupt, convince, coerce, or surreptitiously lure people into our organization.

Even though the finding isn't going to be very difficult, we do have a significant challenge, and it's in the title of this book. Once we find the tribe and make them visible to each other, how do we IGNITE them?

Could we build an invisible tribe into a successor to the companies we have now?

We can, but we must first understand how incredibly uncommon an invisible tribe is at its core—because they are fundamentally different from the organizations of today.

Invisible tribes are decentralized and fragmented, and are often a picture-perfect definition of a motley crew. The people in today's businesses are connected because they need a way to make a living, but this is not the reason an invisible tribe exists *at all*. People join an invisible tribe because they *want to be there*. In an invisible tribe, everyone has opted-in and willingly gives of their attention. They have granted the tribe leaders permission to be part of their lives. They have volunteered their time and discretionary energy. They care deeply about mission and purpose; in fact, many times the group's cause is the primary reason they joined the tribe at all.

In the old world, companies and leaders spent a tremendous amount of time and energy getting enough people to know and care about them, in order to find both employees and customers. But business is now about finding the tribes who *already care*—and then **igniting them**.

Here is the really good news:

Somewhere out there, there is an invisible tribe that wants to help you.

They want to do something *amazing*.

They want to support something *remarkable*.

They want to lend their talents and gifts to a cause that makes a bit of a ruckus, to an endeavor that makes a dent in the universe in some way.

The extraordinary, untapped power of the future of business lies waiting within these invisible tribes. But to tap into their power, we need to adopt a new way of thinking about how to motivate a group.

For the leader, entrepreneur, or change agent who accepts the challenge, there is a tremendous opportunity to help fashion a better way to work.

The only barrier for entry is that we must be willing to become pioneers. We must be grateful for all we've learned about work and at the same time willing to cast off the mooring lines which keep us from sailing forward.

A new kind of organization requires a new kind of leader, and it is the mindset of this trailblazer that is explored throughout this book.

Being a leader, entrepreneur, or agent of change in the emerging economy is about empowering autonomy and inspiring action. It's about designing great environments for the tribe to collaborate within. It's about helping a group leverage their passions and interests and gifts and talents toward a common mission.

Organizations are already uniquely positioned to do these things—they just need to be upgraded to work with the new world instead of against it.

We are on the cusp of a new Cambrian Explosion— and this time it isn't about a staggering emergence of separate individual life, but how individuals are coming back and accomplishing mind-blowing things *together*.

We're not very good (yet) at leveraging the power of the invisible tribes all around us. But take a moment and envision the galaxies of untapped opportunity lying dormant within these communities of passion.

We don't have to find them (recruiting) because they are already finding each other.

We don't have to unnaturally motivate them (compensation) because they work for purpose, not money.

We don't have to trick them to buy (sales), because they desperately want to be part of the larger tribe and will show their support by spending money.

We don't need to prescribe them hours to work (HR), because they *want* to participate alongside a group that gives their life *more* meaning, not less.

We don't have to dictate the best methods for getting things done (operations), because they will be self-motivated to innovate and continually improve our business systems.

Do you see it?

The future of work isn't interruption or coercion; it's finding and igniting.

IGNITION POINT

How can we use these ideas to begin transforming the way we work? Answer the following questions to start a fire of your own:

When I think about the ever-increasing complexity of the world, what is my natural response to this chaotic feeling? Is this feeling helping me thrive?

What am I most passionate about? How can I connect with the tribe of people out there who are also passionate about this? (Some groups are bigger than others, but your tribe is out there, I promise!)

Is the organization I work with life-sucking or life-giving? Why do I feel this way?

In my workplace, do our organizational initiatives focus on individual development more than improving our human systems? How could we improve our human systems?

THE
EXPLOSION
OF
CHOICE

For many centuries—perhaps for all of human history—we couldn't easily access the ideas, the entertainment, the resources, or the other people we needed.

IDEAS

We used to not be able to access the great ideas or information we needed. The best knowledge was contained inside the best professors, in the best schools, in the best libraries, or in the best encyclopedias. If we wanted facts, we had to physically go to those places to get them. *At a personal level: we may have wanted to build something great but couldn't access the information that would teach us how to do it.*

ENTERTAINMENT

We used to not be able to easily access entertaining content. Music was funneled through the major record labels. Films and TV shows were filtered by a few primary television networks and movie studios.

At a personal level: we may have wanted to experience the latest blockbuster but didn't have access to a theater in our 1300-person hometown.

RESOURCES

We used to not be able to access the financial or physical resources we needed. For most people, the local bank was the only real source of potential funding. In terms of physical resources, certain countries are blessed with some and not others, while trade barriers and a lack of efficient and rapid transport made moving these things cost-prohibitive. *At a personal level: we may have wanted to start a business, but had no access to the capital to do it.*

PEOPLE

We used to not be able to access the right people with the strengths and talents we needed to accomplish the kind of work we wanted to do. Inability to efficiently communicate with other parts of the world severely limited our talent reach. *At a personal level: we may have wanted to expand our nonprofit but weren't able to access the right people to do it.*

Limited access to ideas, entertainment, resources, and people drove up their value. Their constrained supply made them precious.

At the same time, this scarcity also centralized a significant amount of power in "top of the funnel" entities like professors (ideas), Blockbuster stores (entertainment), banks or large countries (resources), and big companies with huge recruiting budgets (people).

Business revolves around scarcity because it helps determine what things are valuable, and therefore, what products or services are worth buying. I realize this is Economics 101, but it's important... because it's all about to change *drastically*.

Now, the entire world is at our fingertips—and everything will be even more accessible tomorrow.

What's scarce has changed.

We have more access to ideas, entertainment, resources, and people than we know what to do with. Practically none of what was scarce yesterday is scarce today.

IDEAS

The internet has obliterated any scarcity in our access to ideas or information.[22]

ENTERTAINMENT

Digital media has erased any scarcity of our being able to access quality entertainment.[23]

RESOURCES

Globalization has destroyed any scarcity in our ability to access resources.[24]

PEOPLE

Social networks are rapidly eliminating the scarcity of being able to access the right talent.[25]

This has an enormous impact on business because it makes the funnel virtually irrelevant by eroding the influence of those at the "top" (which these folks naturally find quite unnerving).

It is also completely *opposite* from what we're used to.

In a world where access to ideas, entertainment, resources, and people was difficult, the folks at the top of the upside-down funnel were *very* powerful, because they controlled the communication and the channels of distribution people had to go through to get what they needed.

This allowed ideas like "mass marketing" to thrive—the ability to interrupt great masses of people on a large scale and to impact a large enough population to where a product could almost effortlessly succeed.

In the old world, the "numbers game" worked, and worked *well*. If a marketer could hit enough eyeballs (read: millions—something getting increasingly harder to do) to see their product, a tiny percentage of those would buy it. But a tiny percentage of a huge number is still enough to be profitable.

This is how almost all business aspired to work, in almost every industry. Even the tiniest mom-and-pop shop would have killed to have an advertisement on the hallowed ground of television, for example. In this world, where access to people is scarce and distribution channels are few, the interruption model made quite a lot of sense.

It doesn't make sense anymore.

Business is based on scarcity. That's not going to change. But *what is scarce* changes based on our ability to access it.[26] And access has changed dramatically in the last few decades. New technologies have made information ubiquitous, entertainment digital and free, resources movable, and talent easy to find.

Because of this, customers have more options than ever before.

Great employees have an unprecedented amount of leverage.

Entrepreneurs have a universe of possibilities bursting at their fingertips.

We are just not limited in the ways we used to be.

What happens to business in a world where our choices explode exponentially, and nothing that was scarce yesterday is scarce today?

A work revolution.

THE

WORK

REVOLUTION

When I write and speak, I often use the word "revolution." I know this word conjures up all sorts of images for different people. When I use it, I mean it in the *most literal sense*—as in, once a year the earth makes a "revolution" around the sun.

It's a *complete turn around.*

We're currently experiencing a work revolution, in the most literal way. We are entering a new world where the rules of business have been completely turned on their ear. This is the biggest revolution the world of work has ever seen.

The old way of work is dying, and the sooner we can accept that, the sooner we can find a new way to *live.*

Adopting a new mentality is also a tremendous opportunity for competitive advantage... *for now.* Eventually this different mindset will be the norm, but right now understanding and implementing it is pure untapped opportunity—for those who dare to try something new.

Soon it won't be a choice. When that time comes, we will be left with two options:

1) To ride the changes like a surfboarder on a wave, or

2) To be destroyed by the coming tsunami.

Right now we have an option; the choice is ours.

Most of our fundamental dogmas of work are being challenged. People are looking for a complete re-envisioning of the way we work, searching for a new perspective that integrates work as *part of* a holistic approach to life.[27]

In the new world, work isn't something we merely do for a paycheck, nor is it something that consumes our existence. Instead, it is something that provides us a place to both use our unique genius and also contribute something meaningful to the world.

Some dismiss ideas like these as being too idealistic or even Pollyanna-ish. In truth, it is the only reasonable way forward. If we have the tools necessary to create a better life for the people of the world by designing better businesses, why wouldn't we? Ignoring this possibility is the ridiculous option.

Additionally, research is indicating that companies who adopt a philosophy of "constructive capitalism" or of a more "conscious" way of working routinely perform better from a financial perspective, as well.[28] We also know work environments that create energizing company culture and build on people's strengths are a clear win-win for the people *and* for the bottom line.[29]

Moving forward, the success of our organizations will have a great deal to do with how well we can adopt a new way to work.[30]

The key is to **join** the work revolution instead of fighting it.

IGNITION POINT

How can we use these ideas to begin transforming the way we work? Answer the following questions to start a fire of your own:

What is the thing that is most scarce in my industry? Is that thing actually still scarce today... or am I just wishing it were?

What core need was the business model of my organization designed to meet?

Have any tribes formed around the work I do? If yes, how can I expand and better support those tribes?

If no tribes have formed, why haven't they? Is it possible they are simply invisible to me? How can I make them visible to themselves and to others?

NEW
PROBLEMS

Some people don't like the word "problems."

As a practitioner in the field of positive psychology,
I bump into these people fairly regularly. They prefer
to speak in terms of "challenges," "opportunities," or
"learning moments."

On one hand, this is good. We *should* look at the
opportunity our challenges provide us.

On the other hand, it's a bunch of crap.

When I look at the world as it is, I see some global,
systemic, head-shaking, major freakin' **problems**.

I'm guessing you've noticed some of these, too, or
you'd probably not be reading this.

In this section, we'll explore the new problems
organizations must address if they wish to thrive in the
strange, new, emerging economy.

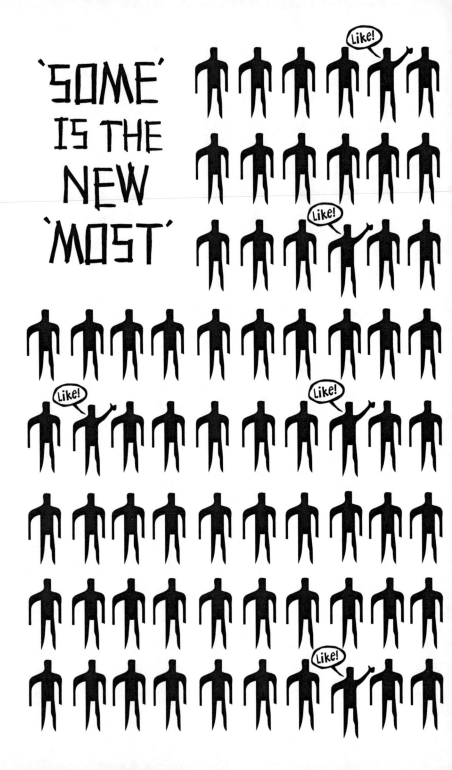

magine I'm a person who likes technology and culture trends and how they impact business. Perhaps I like big-picture issues, I am passionate about sustainability, and I want to somehow change the world.

Hard to picture, I know.

If I am this kind of person and I have something to say about it, in the "old world," if I wasn't lucky enough to be born into a family at the top of the funnel, I would be destined to wander around in my echo chamber until I could get "noticed" by someone "up there" who was benevolent enough to take my message and introduce it to "the mainstream" at the bottom of the funnel.

Admittedly, we often think this is still how it works. But this really isn't the problem anymore, is it? I no longer need the people at the top of the funnel to spread my message. Now, there are the same number of people at *my* fingertips as there are *theirs*.

This takes a moment to grasp, because we've been so steeped in a culture accustomed to big, intimidating, powerful gatekeepers. But it only takes a quick glance online to see the shift; there are solitary Twitter users with followings a major network television show would kill to have.[31]

Because I have the same amount of potential listeners at my fingertips as a major media channel, the TV producer and I have the *same* problem, now:

Most of those "fingertip people" **don't care.**

They really don't.[32]

They don't care what you have to say, and they certainly don't care about what I have to say. *They are only interested in whatever it is they are interested in.*

They are happy to stay in the invisible tribes they're already a part of.

In the scattered, informational-machine-gun world we are in (which will only get more intense), this filtering is an issue of self-preservation as much as it is anything else. As mentioned, we *have* to filter to keep from going crazy. This isn't something to be upset about, however. On the contrary, it's to be embraced—because it helps us know how to move forward.

Note that the word *"most"* is the key word in the alarming sentence above.

Most people don't care.

This means **some** *do*.

It turns out that these "some" care much **more** than the "most" ever would.

In the new world, SOME is infinitely more important than MOST.

And in the new world, it's easier than ever to find the *"some."*

In the emerging economy, we don't have to care about "most,"—*most* isn't where the value lies. In this strange new world, we just need to care about the ones who DO care.[33]

But this is challenging, because most of our current business models are built to appeal to the masses. But these "masses" are quickly being fragmented with each passing day into invisible tribes. *It's the only way we can stay sane.*

The "mainstream," as it used to be, is quickly eroding and will soon be gone, probably forever.

While this is a bit scary for many companies—most of whom have built their institutional power around the upside-down funnel—it's really only scary *up close.*

If we can see this from another perspective, it's a beautiful thing.

LANDSCAPING

In the near-term, these changes do mean uprooting a good deal of our current business practices, and this seems devastating.

But we forget that planting always looks destructive…

…until it's done.

Landscaping is an enormous mess…

…until it's not.

Then it's beautiful.

We must keep our focus on the amazing environment that will come after the chaos.

IGNITION POINT

How can we use these ideas to begin transforming the way we work? Answer the following questions to start a fire of your own:

Am I waiting on any "gatekeepers" I shouldn't be waiting on? What's the first step I can take to give myself permission to move forward?

Have I been ignoring the "some" who passionately care about our product/service because I think the "most" are more important? Who are the "some" that I should pay more attention to?

How can I deepen my relationships with the "some"— understanding that they are the *most important* members of the tribe?

Knowing that things always get messier before they get cleaner, how might I intentionally "create some messes" now which will grow something beautiful later?

THE POWER OF 'INVISIBLE'

Bestselling author Robert Kiyosaki tells a story about a lecture he went to in the 1980's where legendary futurist Dr. Buckminster Fuller was speaking. He says Fuller's message was essentially that "soon millions of people would be... put out of work by technology and inventions that operated well outside their vision."

Dr. Fuller then said: *"You cannot get out of the way of things you cannot see moving toward you."*[34]

I'm guessing you've heard a few stories about people who have recently been "put out of work by technology and inventions that operated well outside their vision."

This is the power of "invisible."

The story of disruptive innovation is an oft-told tale in today's rapidly shifting economy. Amazon replaces Borders. Google replaces Yahoo. Facebook replaces MySpace. Apple replaces music stores. ATMs replace tellers. Automated checkouts replace grocery checkers.

How does this keep happening?

It's actually not that complicated. Essentially, we shouldn't be looking out for the other thing but for the next thing. Disruption happens because what has been isn't replaced by a better version of itself, but by a new product that is *completely different*—and usually markedly better.

In other words, the "old thing" gets replaced by something **revolutionary**, not something *evolutionary*.

It's hard to get out of the way of things we don't see coming—and it's pretty hard to "see" a mindset shift.

To make an ecological analogy, the paradigm change the world is experiencing is much like the physical planet experiencing climate change.[35] In climate change theory, do larger behind-the-scenes changes birth increased storms? Yes, but the storms are *symptoms* of the larger change.

They are the *effect*, not the *cause*.

We see plenty of examples of things that take the blame for today's business crises—new technologies and emerging generations often at the top of the list—but most times these things are *symptoms* of the much larger change. They are not the *cause* of it.

Climate change is also instructive in that much of our natural, physical world is *invisible* to us most of the time. We can't see what's going on in the weather patterns, beneath the oceans, under the crust of the earth, or in the wind. Yet these things all have a *dramatic* impact on our lives.[36]

This hidden, "behind the scenes" change is exactly what's going on in business. People are changing what they expect from work, and consumers are changing what they want from producers.

We want *more* than we did before, but our systems are still built for *less*.

The invisible nature of what's going on is also a big part of why the idea of a "mindset shift" is largely ignored in business. Most of this transition is silently occurring behind the scenes in our perceptions and thought patterns. It's constantly happening all around us, but new ideas move so fluidly and naturally that we don't even notice the change happening—especially when we are overwhelmingly busy, pulled in many directions, and tapped out by jobs that drain our energy.

As discussed earlier, it also doesn't help that most businesses have a significant bias towards the concrete and physical and away from the intuitive and unseen. While tangible is certainly easier, this prejudice is no longer helping us.

Consider the immense power of the following "invisibles:"

- A person's mood, attitude, or intuition
- The foundation of a skyscraper
- A gorgeous song
- The bones in your skeleton
- Highway laws
- The billions of financial transactions processed daily

- A heartwrenchingly beautiful story
- The roots of a giant redwood tree
- The helium inside your child's balloon
- Someone telling you they love you

There is immense strength in things we cannot see, and it is like this in our companies, too. The systems, structures, and cultures that exist in our businesses have an enormous impact on the way we work—but for the most part, we ignore them because they are "outside our vision."

In our organizations we can no longer afford to disregard the power of "invisible."

The entire world is moving from a compartmentalized to a connected mindset (more on this in a few chapters), and this invisible shift is changing business in monumental ways.

The good news is that we do not have to be blindsided by these changes. Once we are aware of the profound shift in mindset happening—and that this is the true cause behind the chaos we feel in the world of work—we can leverage the disruption.

We can learn to use the new rules of work to help us thrive.

Recognizing this transition as the next step of human evolution helps us tremendously, in our personal lives and as leaders, entrepreneurs or change agents. Instead of *fighting to make things work the way they used to*, we can adapt, *change the way we think* and ride the wave.

Sadly, many companies and industries are choosing to fight for the past, instead of the future.[37] This never works, because the future is always fundamentally *different* from wherever we've been.

The way we work isn't getting replaced with a better version of itself, but by something completely new— particularly in what it requires from people.

For a long time it was in the best interest of leaders and managers to keep their workers dumb and happy.

This seems harsh at first, but in a function-driven assembly line world, it's in the best interest of everyone if the assembly line worker stays kind of dumb. The leadership doesn't need a lot of innovative thinking or creativity from a person who's just supposed to press their button all day and go home. Frankly, it's better for the *worker* if they don't want to be a free thinker, because it would only increase their dissatisfaction at having such a crappy job.[38]

It's also good for the company if the person stays content and happy pushing their button. So the business provides just enough perks and benefits to keep them from getting too upset to go anywhere else.

Although, if they do leave we can always replace them; after all, on an assembly line no one is indispensable.

In the old world, life at the top of the upside-down funnel was pretty grand. "Command and control" from the perch is fairly easy and quite practical in this kind of environment.

But over the past fifty years or so this process began to break down. Insightful folks at the top of the funnel noticed that the world was requiring more from their workforce than just "pushing buttons." The marketplace was beginning to yearn for more innovation and imagination. These demands required more complicated processes, and the newly integrated systems demanded that people work together and collaborate frequently.

Company leaders began to need the collective brilliance of the best and brightest minds available. But in order to keep them working at their company, they needed to find ways to inspire those people.

So, being the intelligent, well-paid executives they

were, they began to encourage their employees to get a little *smarter* and a little more *agitated* (goodbye, dumb and happy!).

Thus, the age of training began.

First, employees got smarter. They were sent through training seminars and management programs. They attended workshops and leadership summits. They were encouraged to read books and stay up to date on trade journals. "Go back to school." "Get that MBA!"

Second, employees got agitated. After all, leaders now needed people who were pissed off *just enough* to actually care about making a difference. They needed people who would get upset about poor performance. They needed people who were frustrated enough to spend their discretionary energy on solving the tough challenges—all for the benefit of the company, of course.

So, over the last few decades employees have dutifully become smarter and more agitated, and they have in turn pushed our businesses to new heights of productivity. Unfortunately, while our people *have* evolved… our organizations have not.

They're still built for *dumb and happy*.

We never updated them.

We never really changed *anything* about the industrial factory mindset. We just replaced the overalls with suits and moved people from assembly lines into cubicles.

The list of job duties for an assembly line worker is short and prescriptive: "Push the button." As the workers migrated to their cubes, the list grew longer and got more complex, but still retained its narrow core mindset. It was just an extended list of functions that needed to be performed by the hands, mouths, and minds that were willing to do them.

Instead of pressing a button all day, the office drone now has an overwhelming list of things they're expected to do. In our sophistication we call this complicated, yet still assembly-line-like task list a "job description." We have a "place on the line" for you, too: your desk.[39]

Leaders hire employees under the guise of finding people to "just do what's on their list," but we all know how ridiculous this is. Even though we keep playing the game with everyone else, if anyone were to ask us about *our* job, we would swear that the dynamic, complex, multi-faceted work we do could *never* be ensconced in a list of black and white chores!

And we'd probably be right.

The marketplace *wants* more creativity and imagination. It wants great things to talk about. It wants companies to do remarkable things. These kinds of things, though, are never born out of a list of tasks, but by trying crazy ideas and exploring the "gray areas" between the black and white. They are generated by pushing the boundaries and questioning assumptions.

Essentially, workers are being expected to produce insightful and interesting work, all while being "held accountable" to a dry, static list of tasks that gets stuffed into an HR person's drawer and forgotten five minutes after signing their paperwork—until "performance review time" rolls around, of course.[40]

We tell people to be smart and agitated and then force them into structures that were built for dumb and happy.

The result of this structural confusion is vague annoyance at best, and generates a horrible, toxic environment that makes humans restless and miserable at worst.

I encountered this problem firsthand in my organizational work around employee engagement. During consulting interviews, I would ask a simple question (or rather, a question I thought was simple):

"What do you do in your job that creates value for your organization?"

Now, the funny thing about asking this question, which really isn't funny at all, is that **no one** *seems to know how to answer it*. Unless you count job titles, confused looks, or "I uh, um…" grunting noises as answers. (I don't.)

At first I thought this was simply a poor showing of employees. They weren't prepared, or weren't very bright, or maybe were in the wrong roles. This was a nice theory, but for the most part these were sharp, intelligent people who were good at their jobs.

So why was this question so hard to answer!?

Then I had a strange thought: maybe the problem wasn't *them*. Maybe it was *us…*?

Were we, as leaders, doing all we could to *help* the employees answer this question?

My next thought was this:

*What if it's not even really the leaders, but the way the company is designed? What if we are organizing our companies **around the wrong thing…?***

Is *this* is the main reason why great employees can't answer my "simple" question? Maybe it isn't *them* at all… maybe it's the *structure they're in…?*

As they are built right now, the tribes we call "business organizations"—in any form: small or large, non- or for-profit, and anywhere in between—are built upon the notion of **function**. The very reason we hire people is to fill a specific *functional* role, and each person is hired only to perform that particular *function*.

When a new employee arrives, we give them their list of mostly boring tasks and tell them they are being hired to just do those things over and over and over and over and over and over and over and over again.

The whole process is eerily similar to hiring someone and placing them on the assembly line to push a button all day.

The complexity may have increased, but the box is the same.

In the world of yesterday, it made sense to build a company this way. In the old world (not too long ago, really), processes could be clearly defined and outcomes were predictable. For example, once we learned "how" to build a car, we could break that "how" into procedural steps and then increase the efficiency of that process by removing waste and eliminating redundancies.

But in the chaotic, creative, emerging world of tomorrow, a predictable linear framework doesn't work as well (and often doesn't work at all).

We are moving beyond a function-driven world. But our organizations are still built as if these kinds of tasks are all we do: push "that button," move "this thing" from here to there, put "this" in "that" container.

In the new world, work that is *sequential* is work that is *replicable*. This kind of work will be sold at bargain basement prices to the cheapest bidder in the global marketplace or it will be replaced by machines that can do it better and faster.[41]

But this doesn't mean humans are obsolete. In fact, it means *the opposite*.[42]

Think of Apple, Google, Zappos, Amazon, and Facebook—these are the types of companies that are succeeding most wildly in today's volatile marketplace, and they are breeding grounds for disruptive thinking and creative energy.

The organizational tribes that are finding astounding success right now are companies who are embracing an ethos of continual change and innovation, all *based on the wild imaginations of the people who work there.*

Consumers—me and you—have acquired a taste for this constant newness, and we want more.

We want more of what is *remarkable*.

More of what's *interesting*.

More of the things that are *distinctly, "unreplicably" human*.

The above companies are thriving because they've found a way to work *with* the world's changes instead of against it. They've joined the work revolution, and they're leveraging the power of the invisible. They've found a way to build a structure that, at least partially, allows people to be themselves at their most smart and agitated.

How good are *our* organizations at promoting life-giving work? Work that inspires? Work that is memorable? Work that is fascinating? Work that is meaningful?

If we're being honest, there's not much about our current companies that makes them *more* human. Despite the fact that the very nature of our work has changed dramatically, *the majority of our organizations have not.* Our businesses require some fundamental restructuring.

A function-centric organizational structure is limiting from the outset. When we hire people to only perform within the confines of a specific function we are, in our language and design (even if it's not intentional), limiting their capacity for innovation.

Individuals feel (and to a very real extent, ARE) "boxed in" by the invisible structures of their

workplace, their department, and their job
description.

This outdated structuring is a major reason why
we so often find large-scale change initiatives fail
within organizations. Often, even when individuals
or certain mini-tribes (we usually call these groups
"departments" or "teams") within the larger group
grasp and adopt a particular change, the structures
and systems of the larger organization will remain
a source of constant frustration, "pushing back"
against the change the people were told to make.

This resistance is a direct result of the invisible power
of an organization designed for times that are now
gone.

Many people are *miserable* at work—and if
they're not in outright misery, they're certainly not
there because they really want to be.[43] Outdated
organizational design is a major contributing factor
to this problem. The ability to easily answer the
question "How does what you do in your job create
value for your company?" is at the heart of what
it means to be a happy, engaged employee. *But the*

way we design our companies and hire our employees is
hindering people from answering it.

When the people we talk to at work don't know how
their actions at work create any value, is unhappiness
any surprise?

Given the antiquated nature of our organizational
designs, is it any wonder we're in such a dismal spot?

People *want* to bring their gifts and talents to work.
They want to work on problems that matter and help
society, but our archaic structures "push back" on
this progress.

It's time to upgrade the system.

To do that, we're going to need some new rules.

IGNITION POINT

How can we use these ideas to begin transforming the way we work? Answer the following questions to start a fire of your own:

What does my organization do better than anyone else on the planet?

What is the "big problem" we are trying to solve?

How are new technologies undermining the way we do business now?

How can we change our thinking to not see the above items as "undermining" but instead as fuel to help us ignite new innovations in our company?[44]

NEW
RULES

Whenever people gather together in organized groups—I call them tribes—certain "things" happen. These common behavioral patterns are the specialties of sociologists, anthropologists, and in business, organizational development practitioners.

It doesn't matter if the tribe is for-profit or non-profit, private or public, big or small—any entity that comes together to pursue a common mission by providing an exchange of knowledge, products, or service will always act in certain ways based on the social norms of their group. It follows, then, that if we can affect these rules, we can remake their social agreements—and shift behaviors.

That's why the ideas in this book can have an impact in *any* kind of organization.

Additionally, if the world is changing in fundamental ways, there must also be some fundamental "new rules" which can help us ignite these new kinds of tribes.

In this section, we'll explore what these new rules are.

I n the old world, we needed a lot of laborers.

We needed a lot of people to take "this thing" and move it over to "that place."

We needed people to "press that button" all day.

We needed people to pull and push and expend all sorts of energy doing a whole lot of things... *things most of us just don't do anymore.*

It's not that we won't need those things anymore; it's just that *humans* won't do them much longer.[45] In most places in the U.S., for example, they already don't.

Mail is handled electronically. Buttons are pressed automatically by microchips. Assembly lines are lined with robots. Even forms on websites are filled in for us.[46]

In economic terms, the supply of people who are "good button pushers" has grown much higher than the demand for them.

The demand is going somewhere else.

Innovation and displacement is now happening so quickly, and on such a large scale, that the world is rapidly changing what it needs from workers. The marketplace has clearly declared what it wants now: people who can do creative, connective, collaborative, complex, intelligent work—instead of just "pushing the button."

Many people feel lost in the transition, and understandably so. This tension creates a job crisis that goes much deeper than just having a "job."

We start to question the bigger things... like *why we work at all.*

This is a pretty good question.

Why *do* we work?

At first blush, we'd probably answer: "For the paycheck." While that's partially true—we all need money to live—it's also quite superficial. If we see the purpose of work as to strive for *money*, we've confused the whole idea of **value**.

On its own, money isn't valuable *at all*. Money is only a middleman, an imaginary construct that helps us trade for the things we *truly* value: things like increased freedom, more choices, and better options.[47]

Once we see money for what it is, we see that part of the reason we work is to acquire something (money) that we can exchange for something else we *actually* value, like a place to live, food to eat, or a car to drive.

A better start, but that's still not enough.

Humans are not machines. We don't live to only perform certain functions. We don't exist just to eat and drive and work and sleep. Or, rather, we *shouldn't* (though too many of us do).

It is just **not enough.**

Here's a better definition—still through the lens of acquiring value:

We should work because what we're doing is *valuable to us* and *valuable to society.*

Looking through this lens, the often-nebulous target of "What kind of work should I do?" becomes much clearer.[48] We are simply looking for the intersection between these two points: what creates value for *me* and what creates value for *society*.

The activities that are most valuable to **me** use my gifts/talents/strengths on a regular basis. They give me more energy than they deplete. They make my existence better and not worse. They are life-giving and not life-sucking.

The activities that are most valuable to **society** improve the world in some meaningful way. They make others' lives easier, not harder. They advance the quality of life for some or many people. They do not need to be large-scale initiatives to be important, either. As Mother Teresa said: "It is not how much we do, but how much love we put in the doing."[49]

So, why should we work?

Because it's valuable to me and to society.

Now *that's* a "why" to get behind.[50]

As a leader, entrepreneur, or change agent, we can employ the power of purpose to improve our organization, as well.

In fact, in the new economy, we *must*.

Not only are people searching for greater meaning in their work, but in order to generate the imaginative and innovative results the marketplace is demanding, *we need to help them find it.*

Without a deep connection to purpose, our company won't be able to stay competitive because we will be lacking the authentic commitment and engagement of our people. We must encourage the discovery of "why we work" to happen at both an individual and collective level.

There are many amazing authors and thought leaders who help individuals find their "why." [51] For your group, consider the following questions to get started:

- What is the big problem your tribe is trying to solve?
- How will your company make the world better?
- What hole would be left if your company disappeared tomorrow?

If we wish to thrive in the new world we have to start with *why*.[52]

IGNITION POINT

How can we use these ideas to begin transforming the way we work? Answer the following questions to start a fire of your own:

What kind of work is most valuable to me (it regularly uses my unique gifts/strengths/talents)?

How can I use this kind of work to also produce something that is valuable to larger society?

How can I get paid for doing work that intersects these two points?

RULE #2
BUILD A MOSAIC

For a long, long time we thought we would understand the secrets of the world by studying the smallest pieces of things.

To that end, scientists built bigger microscopes and concocted strange experiments in order to discover the building blocks of atoms.

Doctors and medical researchers peered inside genes to learn about the causes of disease.

Schools divided their learning curriculum into subjects and declared them all equally important for everyone.

Philosophers deconstructed reality to the point of dismantling any sense of meaning.

Financiers split investments into pieces, and then those pieces into pieces (and named those pieces "derivatives"), to further expand their empires.

Fundamentalist religions obsessed over every single letter and punctuation mark, or lack thereof, within their holy texts to try to decipher their "true" meaning.

Lawmakers studied deviant behavior and created police forces, jails, and task forces to deal with crime.

Psychologists reduced the complexities of humanity to a series of disorders and pathologies.[53]

Business leaders partitioned their companies into a series of functional departments and created detailed lists of employee work processes called "job descriptions."

All of this sounds pretty much like "normal" life, doesn't it? This has been our experience for many years. These are all the things we learn in school. For the last few centuries, the human race has been on an unending quest to make sense of the world by studying the smallest pieces of things. We've done it for so long, it almost feels like the only way to live.

But it is *not* the only way to live. It's *not* the only way to think. And it's not even close to the *best* way.

At least, not anymore.

Humanity has gained a great deal of understanding and learned many things through all this reduction and compartmentalization, but we've reached the end of the road with everything on the above list.

SCIENCE
Scientists completed their experiments, peered into their super-powered microscopes and found... nothing. At the "base" of everything is mostly empty space.[54]

HEALTHCARE
Medical science is making progress, but eradicating disease by manipulating DNA is turning out to be much more difficult than we once thought. There's *way* more to a human being than simple building blocks.[55]

EDUCATION
Our schools are starting to feel like obsolete shadows of themselves. The majority of schools in the US are

drastically behind in their learning and scores when compared to the rest of the world.[56] Not to mention that many things we teach our students will be outdated well before they graduate.[57]

PHILOSOPHY

The dismantling of reality via Nihilistic philosophy may be a fun thing to debate over a beer, but is a pretty big failure in practice—people clearly find meaning in their lives in all sorts of ways, every day.

FINANCE

When broken down too far, financial instruments start to look a lot like atoms—a bunch of nothing. When this happens, their value becomes empty, too. Millions who lost their retirement savings in the Great Recession experienced *far* too much of this destructive "derivative effect."

RELIGION

Even when dealing with our most sacred books, it turns out that language is a much more complicated beast than we thought. Something is always lost in translation, and communication is *always* intimately intertwined with context.

LAW/PUBLIC SAFETY

Even something as straightforward as controlling crime doesn't prove to be very simple, as the social environment surrounding the deviant is directly tied to the behavior.[58]

PSYCHOLOGY

Psychologists have realized that positive conduct and excellent living is not the same as just "doing the opposite" of pathology.[59]

BUSINESS

We have Six-Sigma'd our organizations to death. Everyone may not *do* it, but we do know *how* to create efficient processes. Job descriptions are becoming more ineffectual with every passing day as the world becomes more unpredictable. Human beings cannot be automated like machines.[60]

Reducing things to their smallest parts just isn't working like it used to.

Fortunately, a new mindset is rising to take its place. Over the last few decades, a new method of thought has begun to emerge. We're done breaking.

It's time to make a *mosaic* from the pieces.

It's time to put things back together in a way that celebrates the whole picture.

It's time to reclaim the artistry inside us.

As humans, the way we think is changing, shifting. Reducing is just not *enough* anymore. The frontier has moved.

In the new economy, real value is found in discovering *how the pieces connect* and *how they interact.* The ability to create a holistic view of reality is what will make all the difference in the world of tomorrow.

To put it simply, the emerging mindset of humanity is *artistic.* It is a mosaic mindset that makes pictures from the broken fragments. It is the next evolution of human thought, and because of this **an artistic, mosaic mindset describes the way value is created in the new economy.**

If we can adopt this new way of thinking, we can help make work *work* again.

It is accurate to say this new reality is a paradox. We may be shifting to a world of connectedness, but it is connection built from the fragments of yesterday. This is why a mosaic is the perfect metaphor. Taken as a whole it forms a picture, but it is made up of many pieces.

In any industry, across every discipline, a dramatic transformation is at work. From science to healthcare to education to philosophy to religion to law to psychology to business, our thought patterns are migrating. We've successfully extracted all the possible value out of a reductionist mindset.

The brain of tomorrow is connected, holistic—a picture built from pieces.

This perspective helps us understand the new world. Once we begin to recognize that the world now cares more about integration than deconstruction, we begin to value different things in our work. We value collaboration and cooperation. We elevate the importance of artistry and disruption and meaning. We look for prevention instead of treatment of symptoms. We focus on the holistic wellbeing of our people and not just their productivity.

Noticing and learning how to leverage a mosaic mindset is essential to thriving in the new economy. But this isn't easy, because we tangibly see *none of it*. It all happens "in the background," behind the curtains of our mind and behind the scenes of our company culture.

Like they say: awareness is the first step.

When we were living in the "world of pieces," it made *sense* to try to control everything. It's easy to break something down into smaller parts. It's mechanical, and generally speaking, predictable. It's linear and logical: A+B=C. It is an assembly line where we generate a foreseeable result from a set of anticipated variables.

In this world, employees could be dumb and happy and it would be OK. A list of prescriptive tasks kept people occupied in their jobs. A simple trade of time for money was worth it. This is the reality we've been living in.

The world of the mosaic, however, is completely different. It is chaotic and fragmented, but only when we view it *up close*. From further away it is a whole image, a story. It's artistic, and therefore, by its very nature, often unpredictable. It's circular and holistic, a big-picture view of life. Instead of dismantling to understand, we look at how all the pieces fit together in the context of the whole.

In this world, smart and agitated workers are the price of admission—without them, our business is dead in the water. Goals that continually evolve are the norm. People work for meaning as much as money. This is the new world.

The rules of a mosaic world are completely different—as they should be.

The old process, *breaking something into pieces*, requires a wholly different focus from the new process, which is more like *creating a work of art*.

The way we think is moving from a *destructive* perspective to a *constructive* approach.

This is a **monumental** shift.

When viewed in this way, the emerging world starts to make a lot more sense. Think back to the previous list. In a mosaic world, everything looks extremely different.

SCIENCE
Scientists create theories like relativity, quantum mechanics, and entanglements to show the connection and interaction of "empty" objects.

HEALTHCARE
In healthcare, fields like preventive, holistic medicine become more prominent.

EDUCATION
Schools begin to build their core curriculum around connected concepts like "design."[61]

PHILOSOPHY
Philosophers develop insights like social

constructionism, focusing on how humans constantly inject meaning into their environments.[62]

FINANCE

In place of complicated currency, communities begin to create fair trade models, and some groups even organize around trading services and products.[63]

RELIGION

New spiritual movements begin with an emphasis on building bridges between isolated circles of thought.[64]

LAW/PUBLIC SAFETY

To foster safe communities, neighborhood watch programs are created, directly involving the local patrons in security.

PSYCHOLOGY

An entirely new field of psychology is born; dubbed *positive psychology,* it focuses on what's "right with people" instead of obsessing over pathology.[65]

BUSINESS

In business, systems theory and the idea of "synergy"

is born, indicating a recognition that leaders are beginning to recognize that a whole is always *greater* than the sum of parts.

There's a clear pattern here. Everything in the new world is about connection, collaboration, and cooperation. This is the foundation for each of the new rules. Everything is about bringing things that were apart *back together*.

It's about moving from the perspective of a "scientist" to that of an "artist."[66]

This contrast can be a helpful analogy.

The representative figure of the "old world" was the **Scientist**, projecting a reductionistic, mechanistic mindset that deconstructed the world in order to make sense of it.[67]

The representative figure of the "new world," is the **Artist**. Holistic, creative, and purposeful, the perspective of the artist encapsulates what the emerging economy is demanding.[68]

By adopting a mosaic mindset, we begin to see that the way humans view the world around them is shifting dramatically. It's changing from a view of destructiveness (breaking things into pieces) to a generative creativeness (using fragments to form wholeness).

We also begin to see that the worlds of art and business, kept in separate corners for most of the last century, if not longer, are about to come crashing back together.

The collaborative and convergent world of tomorrow is aching for leaders to re-inject *meaning* back into the process of work—and this is something artists do naturally. As more of the world becomes mechanized through globalization and technology, the next frontier of competitive advantage will be filled with things only people can do—and there are few things more fundamentally *human* than art. Furthermore, by helping to foster connections between art and business we're doing our workplaces an enormous service by keeping them relevant—something that great art always is.

How does this impact our organizations?

Instead of approaching work like a series of replicable processes, we will focus on *outcomes*, allowing for and expecting many unique paths to the same result.

Instead of anticipating a product (or business model) to have a long lifecycle, we will treat it like software that should be *continually* updated and improved.

Instead of focusing on short-term profits, we will highlight the impact our decisions will have on *future generations.*

Instead of manufacturing endless copies of mediocre junk, we will strive to be *interesting* and *creative* and *remarkable.*

Instead of making choices that maximize the bottom line at the expense of our people and our planet, we will emphasize the value that our organization adds to the *global community.*

Instead of trying to artificially limit competition we

will *encourage* new ideas in the marketplace, knowing it can only make our organization better.

Connection, collaboration, cooperation.

Holistic, artistic, creative.

The new world is constructed from these pieces. For our organizations to succeed they *must* embrace their inner artist and build a mosaic.

IGNITION POINT

How can we use these ideas to begin transforming the way we work? Answer the following questions to start a fire of your own:

How can we treat our products/services more like software that should be continually updated and improved?

How can we highlight the impact our company's decisions will have on future generations? (*Hint: think about your kids' kids.*)

How can we make our products/services more interesting and creative and remarkable?

How can we emphasize the value that our organization adds to the global community?

How can we encourage competition, knowing it will make our organization better?

How can we focus more on the holistic wellbeing of our people and not just their productivity?

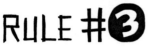

RULE #❸

DIGNIFY
THE
DETAIL DOERS

Everyone alive today has grown up in a business climate where certain kinds of work are viewed as somehow lesser than other kinds.

What this "lesser" work is, specifically, varies from place to place, but it always exists.

In some places it's garbage collectors.

In some places it's golf caddies.

In some places it's administrative assistants.

Wherever it is and whatever it may be, it's a dangerous mentality. *Particularly in the new economy.*

I often speak about creating workplaces where everyone has an opportunity to participate in work that is meaningful. Naturally, people's minds drift towards Google and Zappos and other "progressive" companies, usually in the technology space. Then, these very bright and intelligent people ask me, somewhat hesitantly:

"So... well... how do you create meaningful and interesting work with the more 'unglamorous' jobs? What about toll booth operators?[69] *Or workers who labor in huge factories, processing tomatoes?*[70]

First of all, there's a destructive assumption in the background of this question. This way of thinking assumes that all people don't like that kind of work *just because we don't*. This part is a huge lie. There are people who unequivocally *love* doing the exact kind of work that we unapologetically *hate*. As unnatural as it feels, I see it all the time.

Second of all, there's a dark side to this question (which I'm convinced people don't mean), which lessens the importance of those jobs *simply by asking the question*. We've already made up our minds that those jobs are unglamorous and *can't be anything but*.

This part isn't necessarily true either, although in many cases we've made it so by believing it.

For us to be able to collaborate efficiently—which is what the new world demands—we simply cannot have these kinds of working prejudices. It destroys our ability to form relationships with the complementary partners we need most. Collaboration, at its core, is about balance. It's about someone else being strong where we are weak. We can't appreciate or leverage this when we carry around blanket assumptions about some types of work being "lesser than"—especially because it is those kinds of workers we probably need the most.

Part of this challenge is easy to understand. There is a natural human response that makes us believe the things we do not personally understand are somehow *lesser* in value. For example, if I do not particularly enjoy swinging a hammer, I naturally think that everyone else *ought not* like that either.

However, the same could be said for the construction worker who derives a great deal of meaning by building things with their hands, and cannot understand why a person could *possibly* want to sit in meetings and talk about strategy all day.

We all define ourselves as what's "normal," even if we think we don't.

This tendency to define our world as a reflection of our own worldview is a natural mechanism of the human psyche. It's even partially good, because it provides us with our own unique talents and perspective and passion and drive. But it can also be incredibly *limiting* if it keeps us from understanding (or at least respecting) how other people can truly care about different things than we do.

In the emerging economy, it is essential for us to allow others the freedom to create meaning in whatever kind of work they see fit. It's not our job to judge what someone else should or should not find meaningful. In order to succeed in the emerging marketplace we must fight the urge to project our own tastes on others, because *we need those people who are different,* now more than ever!

In a world built around collaboration, those who are most different from us are the very ones who can make us most successful.

This understanding translates to a group, as well.

At the heart of an invisible tribe is a recognition that any particular tribe, whatever it may be organized for, is passionate about *something*. For that tribe to be ignited in the business marketplace, however, the community must recognize the interlocking connectedness of its own group with other tribes *who can do the things they can't.*

Due to their specialization—by definition, an invisible tribe is focused on a particular "thing"— each community *needs* other communities in profound ways. Additionally, in an ironic twist, an invisible tribe will only be able to truly focus on what *it* is passionate about when it **allows others to do the same.**

This is another reason why a mosaic mindset is so helpful in the emerging economy: it helps us appreciate the beauty of contrasts. In a mosaic, the only reason a picture emerges is because of the different colors and shapes of the pieces. Without the variety and balance, we'd just be looking at a plain, blank wall. It simply doesn't *work* without the diversity. The new marketplace is the same: hyper-connected and inter-dependent.

I realize that is still fairly conceptual, so how do we make this approach a bit more actionable?

To that end, there is a simple idea that can help us move along the path towards more generative, meaningful work.

Interestingly, it has almost nothing to do with how we act *at work*. Instead, it has everything to do with how we act towards those who are *working around us* all the time.

This idea is called "The Dignity Test," and it goes like this: in every interaction you have with a "service person"—this includes passing a Target employee in the aisle, seeing a janitor sweep the floor at the Apple Store, or peering over the glass at Starbucks as the barista pours your latte—make a conscious note to check what you're thinking.

Particularly look to see if you're thinking anything *about them*.

The next part is to make sure that, in our perception of them, **we dignify them**. We should ensure we are thinking of them *as a human being*, not just as the device which delivers the thing we're buying, or the broom and dustpan which lifts the garbage off the ground, or the machine which keeps us caffeinated.

Far too often we see the workers as being as disposable as the consumable we're purchasing.

Harsh? Yes.

True? Afraid so.

Even though we know better, our perceptions are damaged. We unconsciously see some jobs as "lesser," and this transfers into how we view the *people* who do those jobs.

We don't mean to, but it happens quite often.

We need a dignity test for how we think about people who have jobs we'd never do. We must constantly be aware, and adjust, our perceptions of the workers around us.

Correcting these perceptions is crucial for our own leadership and our own organization, because in our workplace there will certainly be jobs we view as somehow "lesser" than ours. But they are not. We can't *begin* to comprehend how **anyone** would want to do those things—*but they do.*

In a world that's becoming increasingly cooperative, viewing everyone as a potential partner is a much more helpful, productive, and profitable mindset. The people performing jobs outside the scope of what we enjoy are *exactly the people we need the most.* But we can't truly work with them unless we respect them.

Remember that in the emerging economy "working with" means leveraging the unique strengths of the other person.

When we adjust the way we think about the people we meet *outside* of our work, it helps us do the same *in our own workplace*—and will get us one step closer to designing a life-giving company culture.

I had an instructor in grad school say, "*Always remember to dignify the detail doers.*"

Yes, that pretty much sums it up.

IGNITION POINT

How can we use these ideas to begin transforming the way we work? Answer the following questions to start a fire of your own:

What can I use as an "internal trigger" that will remind me to treat the workers around me with dignity?

How can I create more space in my daily life to "zoom out," in order to have more time to reflect on the bigger picture and what is most meaningful about my work?

What can I do to help me see my work more as an art?

What are three ways I can use more of my inherent creativity at work?

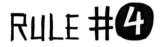

RULE #**4**

MAKE LIKE
A
SHARK

&
SWIM

Human beings have not only the *capacity* to grow and change, we seem to have a *need* for it as well. The opportunity to grow and develop is a crucial component of employee engagement, for example. Despite this, most organizations seem to have an astonishing amount of hatred for change.

This won't work, moving forward. We need to find a way past our distaste for change. After all, the world is *not* going to stop evolving.

For at least the last eighty years or so, our business institutions have seemed relatively stable.[71] In this world, change seemed to come at a manageable pace.

This isn't the case anymore, and it is one more reason why it's helpful to think of business like art.

Look at the world of fashion. When it comes to the art of making clothes, we *expect* that certain clothes will drift "in style" and then sometime later "go out of fashion." This may annoy us, but we are not surprised by it.

Or think of music. All music exists because of the myriad sounds that came before; it's cumulative and progressive. While some music may seem to be "timeless," like all art, music is at its most powerful when it builds on the shoulders of giants, while portraying a new message that is timely and relevant.[72]

Art by its very nature is designed to interact with current events and the world that is currently at our fingertips—the world that is incessantly, ceaselessly changing.

Making our organizations work in this kind of world isn't as much about *speed* as it is about *timing*. To be sure, the world is faster now than it used to be.[73] Our technologies have reduced our attention spans, and "slow" seems to mean something different than it used to. But again, if we leverage a mosaic perspective we see that it's not about unending acceleration—it's simply about *having the right thing for the right time.*

Let's return to the art analogy. The most powerful music is tied to a specific time—it makes the most sense in a particular context. It is most meaningful when understood in the environment it was written in. This is the same with literary art and visual art.

Our organizations are like these kinds of time-bound art—they meet a specific need with their specific product for a specific time. Because of this, what they do must be constantly evolving, never static.

*And we have to work **with** this reality, not against it.*

I'm sure none of this surprises you. It's the *sustaining* of all the constant change that is so difficult, after all. Because of the incredible way that the world is connecting, we're now competing with more people and companies than we ever have before. This means change that is continual and incredibly intense. And this need for progress and evolution is going to get much, much worse (or better, depending on your perspective!).[74]

The only way forward is to make change a part of our business model. We need to weave it into our work lifestyle.[75]

This is a challenge, because many individuals I talk to are change-averse, as well. And even if they're not, they either feel like they are *supposed* to be or they've learned to avoid it—usually for good reason. Particularly in organizations, change **sucks**. But this isn't because the *change* actually sucks.

It's because the organization sucks at changing.

When a group can't evolve, it makes change miserable for everyone involved. If you've had the "joy" of experiencing a large organization "change management" effort, you know I speak the truth.

To move forward, we first have to make peace with the *idea* of change. We have to shake its hand and realize that it is not our enemy, but our friend. In fact, there is something fundamentally *human* about change.

Think of your life as a book, cover-to-cover, beginning to end, birth to death. When reading a book, we don't just read the same page over and over; we'd never get anywhere! But in many ways, that is the way we often try to live our lives, and consequently the way we run our organizations. We find a nice, comfortable page and we try to stay on it. Or in business, we find a sales model that *worked* and assume it will always *work*. We read that one chapter over and over and over and over...

But life doesn't work like that. Business doesn't work like that. We are *meant* to turn the page. We are *designed* to change.

The truth is, without change, we die. Literally.

Everything about us as human beings exists in this suspension-bridge tension between birth and death. We live in the gray, somewhere between degeneration and regeneration. In fact, every second approximately one million of the cells in your body die.[76]

Every second.

When you read that—"*Every second*"—a million more cells kicked the bucket. Gone. Kaput.

But you're not disappearing.

This is because your body isn't *just* dying; it is also constantly *creating*. It creates new cells constantly; the marrow inside your bones, for example, produces **250 billion** new red blood cells every single day.

We exist in this space between birth and death, between regression and progression.

If we want to keep living—and if we want to keep our organizations alive and thriving—we *must* change. Standing still is not an option. (It never really has been; it just used to be easier to ignore.)

Like a shark that can only breathe if it keeps swimming, our organizations must continue progressing, innovating—*changing*—if we desire for them to stay alive.

Growth, innovation, expansion, development, maturation, evolution, progress, advancement—these are all treasured expressions to describe value-adds to businesses on résumés, but they are actually synonyms for just one word:

Change.

Then why do organizations find change so terrifying?

Seth Godin makes a great point about this. He states that from an evolutionary perspective, organisms are change-averse because change signifies risk, and risk indicates danger. Even though our brains still register this fear as intensely as if we were being chased by a saber-toothed tiger, most risk we face isn't life-threatening—it just feels like it.

But in the new economy, we don't have the option to *not change.* Change has become an expected part of what the marketplace demands. Customers like me and you constantly want new, better, more exciting, more extraordinary, and more awesome. Old is boring and outdated.[77]

Luckily for all of us, we have **a clear opportunity** and **a new best practice** that will help us ingrain change into our company cultures.

A Clear Opportunity: Emerging Generations

Emerging generations don't know anything *but* constant change. They just assume that the apps on their iPhones are going to be updated and improved every couple months—in the *least*. We don't even have to teach these individuals how to be this way!

What we will have to do, however, is to re-imagine how to structure our organizations to initiate an atmosphere of continual growth, so these extraordinary individuals will be able to *keep swimming*.

We've all heard the adage that the only thing truly certain is change, and in a way, this has always been true. But the younger members within the emerging culture have had an ethos of change thrust upon them from the moment they were born. Look back over the last thirty years and make a list of significant cultural changes. The catalog is mind-boggling.

For the newest members of the workforce, the continual change happening now is *not* crazy. To them, it doesn't even seem like *that* much evolution— it is *simply the way life works.* They *expect* change—and if it is not there, your best star employees will try to *create* it.[78]

But if our organization's structures aren't built to openly embrace that change, the culture will crush the tension at the source. Our company will lose its best new talent, and the organization will eventually start a death spiral.

We know we *need* change for our companies to stay alive—to grow, to *thrive*—and we now have an enormous group of individuals predisposed to help create it. Are we taking advantage of this?

. . . . .

A New Best Practice: Forever-Beta Everything
Our organizations also fear change because we have long believed there was "one right way" to do something. We thought there would be "one correct final product" with "one correct path" to get there. In this world, any *change* implicitly meant we were *wrong*.

Nobody likes to be wrong.

Fortunately for leaders, with an adoption of a new approach to product development this too is becoming an outdated mentality.

For an example, let's examine Google. Many times, Google would first release their products and services to a limited number of people who would help the company iron out bugs and ready the product to be ready to scale. Gmail, for example, was labeled as a "beta" product for so long that it actually became somewhat of a joke in the "tech community" (which is really just an invisible tribe of nerds like me who make jokes about things like Gmail). But essentially, what Google is doing is *crowdsourcing their product development.*[79]

The early adopters who test the beta versions of the new product have different *expectations.* They not only don't mind the problems, they actually *use their own time to help the company solve them.* These beta testers are not on Google's payroll, but they are certainly providing Google a service!

Guess the joke was on us.

What we are seeing here is a new model for product lifecycle and customer engagement, one that intimately involves consumers as active participants in the creation and development of new products, and it works because the organization is **tapping into their invisible tribe**, not "paying for market research."

In the new world, change *isn't* viewed as failure. Change is seen as continual, progressive improvement.

Change is just the way life works.

Maybe Google's "forever-beta" projects are closer to the way we should see *all* our products and processes. Maybe we should see our **organizations** this way, too. Maybe we'd be better off if we saw *everything* as never done—never as good *as it could be*. Maybe our love for a "final product" has been a contributing factor to our inability to continually innovate?

· · · · ·

Organizationally speaking, what if we are simply coming at the issue of "change" from the wrong side? What if, instead of trying to fashion an organizational structure that strives for "the one way it must be done," we could build the idea of *change, learning, and growth* into the very fabric of the company?

What if the notion of change could actually be *part of the structure?*

What if we give every single employee permission (and a tangible infrastructure) to create and submit innovative ideas? What if we did this for each of our *customers?*[80] Can we even imagine how much *better* we could get?

If you've not seen examples of this, it may seem like the most outlandish suggestion in the world. But this very idea is one of the main strategies behind the Toyota Production System, which made Toyota one of the most successful and respected organizations in the world.[81]

Additionally, as you're reading this, there are literally hundreds of entrepreneurs racing to create social software for the workplace which will allow any business to capitalize on wisdom that can come from anywhere inside or outside the organization.[82]

The tools are never the hard part, though.

The difficulty lies in execution.

I wish I could say integrating a mentality of change is going to be easy to implement in every organization. I wish I could wave some kind of magic wand, throw fairy dust in your face, snap my fingers and have your leaders, managers, and employees understand the implications and benefits of integrating these ideas. But I have spent significant time in many organizations, and I have yet to find *one* where the fight for excellence is anything but just that: a battle.[83]

But I don't have to tell you that some things really *are* worth fighting for.

I'll also say the organization that does not make continual evolution part of their DNA will almost certainly not be around in ten years.[84]

So make like a shark—and swim.

IGNITION POINT

How can we use these ideas to begin transforming the way we work? Answer the following questions to start a fire of your own:

How can I help my organization better leverage the power of emerging generations to create and sustain a culture of change?

How can I help my organization involve our customers to a greater extent in the continual development and evolution of our products/services?

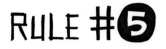

RULE #5

BE CONNECTED, HUMAN, & MEANINGFULL

Through my research, I studied many companies: small and big, old and new, in all sorts of industries and disciplines. I explored everything from higher education to government agencies to non-profits to the private sector. I visited small mom-and-pop operations and big family business. I listened to leaders in mid-size organizations and had lunch with managers in Fortune 100 companies. I studied with some of the top researchers in the world and read literally hundreds of books, blogs, and articles.

As I began connecting the dots, clear patterns emerged. Companies succeeding in remarkable ways in today's volatile economy were always doing *something* that fit into one of three larger groupings. They were deliberately architecting their environments in a few distinct ways.

For a tribe/organization/group/company to build a life-*giving* work environment (instead of a life-*sucking* one) in the new world, their actions must be at least one of three things:

1) Continually *Connected,*
2) Distinctly *Human,* and
3) Purposefully *Meaningful.*

These three words represent a set of "guiding principles" of the new mosaic world.

Connected, Human, and **Meaningful.**

Being **Connected** is the recognition that what I do affects you—or, as a tribe, what *"we"* do affects *"them."* It's about fostering sustainability, both from an environmental standpoint and from a human perspective.

Being **Human** is all about treating people like real human beings. People are complex and unique creatures with passions and emotions and strengths and stories. The work environment of the future *"gets"* this and amplifies its benefits.

Being **Meaningful** is helping the people in the tribe connect to something bigger. It's about purpose and mission—and I don't mean "statements." It is the driving force "behind the scenes" that powers intrinsic motivation.[85]

Think back to the explosion of choice we are now experiencing (from the *New World* section). Because the things that used to be scarce are not anymore, doors previously closed to us have now been blown wide open. We have options we've never had before, but the laws of scarcity still apply. The unasked question from that section was:

What's scarce in this strange new world?

This the other way to look at the three guiding principles of being Connected, Human, and Meaningful—in the emerging economy, *they* are the things which are scarce. This makes them immensely valuable for the foreseeable future.

If you're searching for a way to connect your career or organization to these shifts—and wish to join the revolution instead of fighting it—explore the following:

BE CONNECTED

The need for things that connect us to each other will grow exponentially in the coming decades.

Technology that does this is already booming, of course. Practically every tech startup we hear about is exploiting this principle, and it's precisely why many of them are succeeding. From Airbnb to Instagram to Path, the leverage points of these services lie in the links. The market valuation of many of these companies shows that in the emerging economy, helping connect people to each other is *enormously* valuable.[86]

As we've discussed, the world of the upside-down funnel was easier from a communication perspective because it wasn't nearly as chaotic. In that climate, any messages we heard were limited and generally focused. But we now live in a world where everyone has a megaphone, so we've constantly got a cacophony of voices to filter out. This makes connections to people we truly listen to—and to leaders and groups we listen to—more valuable than ever before. We welcome these filters because we *need* them, and with each passing day it's becoming easier to find and connect with our trusted tribe. These connections, and the services that enable them, will continue to grow exponentially.

Being connected also has to do with connecting the actions we take *today* to the results we get *tomorrow* (or, on the darker side, the consequences we will have to live with tomorrow). At its core, sustainability is really about connectedness. It's an understanding that what I do affects you—or, as stated above, knowing that what *my* tribe does can dramatically impact the way *your* tribe gets to live. This means products or services which improve the sustainability of processes, organizations, and people will be in high demand—because right now businesses that have anything resembling this kind of balance are incredibly scarce.[87]

This yearning for greater connectedness is playing out on a global scale. When we have the space to reflect, we know the logical conclusion of insatiable consumerism won't create the world we want for our grandchildren. We instinctively understand that our wasteful behavior should not continue.[88] The connectedness of the new world is pushing us in a better direction. We *can* find ways to generate products that can be endlessly re-used and re-cycled—if we desire to do so.

COMPANY	Why They're "Connected"
FACEBOOK	At the time of writing, Facebook had over 900 million people in its network, making it the clear global master of pure, literal connection.[89]
PIKE PLACE FISH MARKET	In the world of fish markets, not harming habitats in any way or depleting populations by overfishing is incredibly rare, and Pike Place is committed to being 100% sustainable in these ways.[90]
SEVENTH GENERATION	The mission on their website states they exist to "inspire a revolution that nurtures the health of the next seven generations." Depending on how you measure it, that's at least 200 years. So much for sticking to quarterly reports.[91]

BE HUMAN

The need for systems that improve the human aspects of business will become even more essential in the coming years.

As the work we do gets more complex and nuanced, it will become essential for workplaces to provide liberating structures where people can be energized and motivated. Without this, company owners and leaders will miss out on the discretionary energy of their employees—and this is precisely the energy that creates the best and most cutting edge, innovative stuff.

Additionally, in the near future, all work that can be done by machines likely will be. This will happen sooner than we realize, and when it does all repetitive tasks will be relegated to technology. In this kind of world, activities that can be performed *only by human beings* will be at a premium.

Please don't interpret that statement as being scary or dystopian; I'm not envisioning the opening scene of *The Terminator*. In reality, the activities that can only be done by people are often the things we enjoy most.[92] This includes things like creativity, design, inspiration, delighting customers, innovation, communication, craftsmanship, performance, solving complicated problems, inventing new solutions, and art.

In the new world, being human—and creating workplace systems that allow people to tap into their creative selves—is no longer a "nice to have," but a categorical imperative.

COMPANY	Why They're "Human"
ZAPPOS	By offering new employees cash on the spot to quit, building all systems around good employees (instead of the troublemakers), and insisting on the continual creation of "fun and a little weirdness," Zappos literally treats their call center employees like kings and queens.[93]
MORNING STAR	One of the largest processors of tomatoes in the world (over $700 million in revenues), Morning Star is unorthodox to say the least. They have no managers, peers decide compensation, and anyone can spend the company's money.[94]
SAS	With jaw-dropping perks including unlimited sick days, free on-site health care, and a 66,000 square foot exercise facility, SAS truly treats employees like their "most valuable asset."[95]

BE MEANINGFUL

The need for people who help us connect to a greater sense of meaning in our lives will be crucial in the new economy.

Finding inspirational ways to help connect people with their purpose has never really gone out of style, but in a world that is increasingly fragmented, we will need many more artisans who can build "mosaics" from the "pieces." Our world is becoming more fast-paced than ever before, and shows no signs of slowing. This means finding ways to help people slow down and create balance from an increasingly topsy-turvy lifestyle will be invaluable.

Also, I am not necessarily talking about religion or spirituality here (though that will certainly be vital to some). As we've discussed, the research indicates that people are increasingly looking for purpose *within* their work. They want to be connected to *something* bigger than themselves. Meaningful work does this, and counter-intuitively, our workplace is actually the *best* place to find meaning—after all, where do we spend more time?

In an organization, being meaningful has much to do with the creation of structures that allow people the space to reflect and recover. When we have no rhythm, we quickly disconnect from a greater sense of purpose.[96]

In whatever field you're passionate about, you can meet a deep need in the emerging economy by being a meaning-maker.

COMPANY	Why They're "Meaningful"
APPLE	Something about Steve Jobs' desire to "put a dent in the universe" seems to have embedded itself in Apple's products. There are few companies (or celebrities, for that matter) that have "fans" this excitable.[97]
TOMS	By embedding one-for-one gifts into their business model, a simple shoe company inspired meaningful copycats everywhere and has delivered over 1 million pairs of desperately needed footwear to kids around the world.[98]
SEMCO	This hierarchy-free organization has been treating people like adults for decades, allowing them to find their purpose by "retiring a little," switching jobs as life changes, and, of course, determining their own daily schedules.[99]

Interestingly, the tribes I studied aren't *intentionally* organizing around these guiding principles. They don't realize what they're doing fits clearly into one of these three larger categories. But even though they don't know it, whatever is working for them invariably makes them **Connected, Human,** or **Meaningful.**

It's also worth noting that no single company I've studied is leveraging all three principles… *yet.* This means that right now, being **Connected, Human,** and **Meaningful** is a *massive* competitive advantage. Adopt them *now* and your organization will be on the cutting edge.

But I have to warn you, this advantage won't last long.

Soon, every organization will adopt these practices— they won't have a choice if they wish to keep up.

Our emerging culture is looking for a complete re-envisioning of business. We are searching for a new kind of organization: one that can adopt a more holistic approach. We are yearning for work that connects us to each other, treats us like human beings, and provides us a greater sense of meaning.

When a tribe finds success in the emerging economy, it is because they have found a way to bring at least one of the three guiding principles of a mosaic world to life. They are intentionally **Connected**, they are deliberately **Human**, or they are making life more **Meaningful**.

That's it.

IGNITION POINT

How can we use these ideas to begin transforming the way we work? Answer the following questions to start a fire of your own:

How can I be more "connected" in the work that I do (more sustainable, more future-focused, more aware of the consequences of my behaviors)?

How can I be more "human" in the work that I do (give more dignity to those around me, more effort to learn people's stories, pay attention to the strengths of others)?

How can I be more "meaningful" in the work that I do (remember the true end-user impact of my work, slow down for recovery and reflection, join a tribe that better aligns with my passions)?

NEW TOOLS

We can envision things we can't yet create.

In 1989, Disney animators wanted to create a film about a mermaid with wild, red, curly hair. Unfortunately, as Wired magazine reports, "rendering that kind of bounce and frizz, cel after hand-drawn cel, was all but impossible."[100] In 2012, twenty-three years later, thanks to new hair simulation technology designed at Pixar, a heroine protagonist with fiery red, curly locks will finally get her movie debut in *Brave*.

In 1996, James Cameron announced that he was going to make a film called Avatar, but the technology did not yet exist to make it a reality.[101] The film was finally released thirteen years later in 2009, with Cameron's team inventing much of the technology needed to create the film's otherworldly effects.

In order to create something that's never been built before, we need new tools.

In this section, we'll explore the new tools required to ignite invisible tribes, including new language, new categories for workers, a new dominant organizational metaphor, new approaches to organizational rules, and a new way to physically structure an organization.

ARCHITECTS & BUILDERS

The Integral Institute is a think tank in Colorado that was founded in 1998 by author and holistic psychologist Ken Wilber.[102] In addition to many other things, the Integral team has embarked on a fascinating project: essentially, to take the last hundred-ish years or so of human behavioral science and comb all of it for patterns. (Yes, *all* of it.) By taking all this data and layering it all on top of each other, they've been able to analyze the "meta" patterns that exist within the data and see where the common insights from these varied perspectives lead.

As reported in the book *Tribal Leadership*, one of The Integral Institute's most fascinating findings is in regards to the power of language. Wilber reports that there are essentially two parts of a human being that progress in stages together: their *mindset/ philosophy/worldview* and their *conversations*.

The implications of this are profound. I'm sure there

are others, but for me this means two things:

1) We can monitor the internal, hard-to-quantify development of people simply by listening to their conversations, and

2) If we can authentically influence the way a person talks about the world around them, we are quite literally *changing the way they think.*

We are only beginning to realize the potential that exists here, particularly in our organizations.

In our companies, we are generally pretty good at crafting an external public-facing brand and an integrated marketing message that inspires and motivates people to action.

Internal corporate communication, on the other hand, is often the most dry, boring, lifeless drivel a human being can ever be so unfortunate as to lay their eyes on.

For something that has the power to change the way people think, we're missing an *enormous* opportunity here. [103]

If we are trying to build organizations that do the opposite of suck, perhaps we can use the wisdom of The Integral Institute and leverage the powerful tool of language to help?

In most work tribes, we have a popular dichotomy: "leader" vs. "follower." In this largely unspoken arrangement, the leaders do the *thinking* and the followers do the *doing*. The leaders are *higher* on the ladder and the followers are *lower*. The leaders are paid *more* and the followers are paid *less*.

This hierarchy doesn't make sense anymore.

Now that the funnel has been flattened, the "followers" have an enormous impact on the brand because they actually make the stuff people buy and have the direct personal access to customers. In an age where distribution is decentralized and people have a nearly infinite variety of options for spending their time and money, this asset—a personal connection to products and customers at an emotionally engaged level—is one of the most valuable things a company can have.

This means that in the emerging economy, the priorities our organizations are built to reinforce—hoards of marginally-paid followers "led" by the über-rich fat-cats "above" them—are *backwards*, and are quite likely harming our business. There may need to be more people in the "follower" category than the "leader" category from a quantity perspective, but we can't allow that to diminish the dignity of this essential group.

In a mosaic world, both groups desperately need each other because they have extremely different strengths.

This presents a fundamental problem, however, because as our organizations are structured now, there's no way for this relationship to exist except in hierarchy.

It's been said that words create the world.[104] Perhaps, then, we can create a better world of work by using a few new words.

First, the former "followers." Instead, let's call them **"BUILDERS."** They are the makers, the creators. They *do* stuff. *Great stuff.* Their work is essential, because without them, *nothing ever happens.*

Second, the former "leaders." Instead, let's call them "**ARCHITECTS**." They are the managers, the designers. They draw the plans and create the strategies. And this work is crucial, because without them, the *wrong stuff* might get built.

In the new world, the job of Architects is to provide places for groups of Builders to perform their most excellent work. Their natural strengths allow them to focus on strategy and the future. They get energy by designing work environments that allow Builders to work to their highest and most creative potential. They fashion structures that celebrate the creation of brilliant, collaborative work.

In the new world, the job of Builders is to build remarkable things to ensure the Architects' best ideas can get translated into reality. Their natural strengths allow them to execute efficiently and flawlessly. The things they "build" might be fabulously sticky relationships or aesthetically perfect products, but their work is excellent and demands to be dignified.

In the new world, both of these groups exist on a
level playing field. They are equal partners. One is not
"higher" or more important to the process. Like the
parts in a play, each role is essential to the plot—and
each character requires a unique set of strengths.[105]

This lack of hierarchy will be difficult for most of us.
We've been thoroughly conditioned to only think
in competitive terminology. But like so many items
from the reductionist "old world," this is a zero-
sum game—one person wins only when someone
else loses. We no longer have to work this way, and
frankly, this mindset has reached its limit in terms of
productivity. The emerging economy demands that
we re-think the way we structure, and language is a
perfect tool to help us get started.

In the business world we are emerging from, jobs in
the Builder category are consistently demoralized,
minimized, and deglamorized. These are the "detail
doers" who are not dignified. In the new world,
however, this category of worker is unquestionably
equal to an Architect. The entire power structure has
flattened.

New terminology can help us recreate the world around us. Language is powerful, and these new labels can be the foundation that provides the structure for our new framework.

You've probably heard the phrase, "the devil's in the details."

While the alliteration is lovely, we've got it wrong.

Whatever our conception of the divine may be, it's *GOD* we find in details, not the devil.

There is much discussion about "company culture" these days—how to create it, sustain it, manage it, and influence it. This dialogue is certainly moving our companies in the right direction; the idea of "culture" is just a bit slippery. What we call *culture* is an extremely complex amalgamation of rituals, customs, mores, and systems. It's continually influenced by the Architects and Builders that live within it, from all sides at the same time. It's a natural, organic outgrowth of many different factors within the tribe's ecosystem.

However, where culture is an intricate and unwieldy thing to harness, *environment* is something we can build. We already know how to design buildings, spaces, and *environments* that make sense and give people energy.

Instead of trying to directly impact something as complex as culture, then, maybe we'd be better off designing the environment that will produce the culture we want?

In the natural world, if we build the proper ecosystem we can grow most anything. It's like this in our business cultures, too.

This is why organizational architects must see that they are truly *environment architects.*

To be clear, when I say "environment" I'm not talking about the world of the outdoors; this isn't a chapter about trees or mountains or weather patterns. By "environment" I simply mean *all the things that surround us.*

In our companies, then, *environment* is everything
from how much light comes through the windows…

to the technology we're allowed to use at work…
to the performance review we use…
to how we conduct our meetings…
to the paint on the walls…
to the dress code we require…
to the way we respond to "the numbers"…
to the working hours we mandate…
to the cleanliness of the room we're in…
to the layout of the desks in that room…
to the stories we tell…
to the colors in the logos we use…
to the "stuff" that goes in our email signatures.

Everything.

This is environment, and most of the time these
things don't get a *first* thought (much less a second)
in our businesses—at least not in regards to the fact
that *these are often the very things* which either **give us
energy or suck it out.**

Sounds dramatic? It's not.

If you are tending a garden, does the amount of light matter?

If you are watching a movie, does the comfort of the seats matter?

If you are attending a concert, does the right volume matter?

If you are designing a website, does the white space matter?

If you are in a jail cell (or an office), does a window matter?

Little things are *never* little.

God is in the details.[106]

The environment we create around ourselves is the tangible expression of our values. We are continually reinforcing the things that truly matter to us, and disregarding the rest.

A workplace environment is a highly complex ecosystem, and we often give it less attention than the flowers we forget to water at home.

Both groups—Architects and Builders—are responsible for generating a life-giving work environment.

Great Architects design everything down to the minute details, knowing they all matter.

Great Builders pride themselves on executing precise work, because they know the details matter.

Throughout human history, this is how all great structures have been built—architects and builders working together to design an environment that is (hopefully) life-giving. The push and pull between designers and doers is where the magic really happens. Of course, in the past we've not done very well at recognizing the equality of these two kinds of workers. Moving forward we can design ecosystems that dignify both crucial parts.

In an organization, our environmental choices

either give people more life or they suck it out. *They can't do both.* This is why it is so important that we *intentionally* design our work environment, and that we execute those plans *well*.

All living beings are profoundly impacted by their environment. We know this is true in the communities where we live—we can see this fact reflected in crime rates, in safety statistics, and in studies of wellbeing.[107] But even though we "know" this, staggeringly little time, attention, or money is given to deliberately building an environment that actually promotes *life* at work.

What kind of environment are you building?

As mentioned, environment is the tangible expression of values—and values, of course, are invisible. That makes this kind of work seem difficult, but there is an easy clue to follow. The best way to "see" your values is to look around at the culture it's producing—look at the "crops" that are growing.

Is your ecosystem producing happy, energized, creative, engaged workers? Is the environment you've built a place where people can do their most creative, important, and passionate work? Can workers bring their whole, human selves to their job and be rewarded for it? Are employees able to connect what they do every day with some larger purpose?[108]

Now, the execution (the really tricky part).

How many great employees do you know who have a lot of "free time" when they're on the job? (Remember, I'm not talking about the lazy people. I said the "great" ones.)

If you're like me, not many.

The great people are almost always busy—their work ethic is well respected, and this is a big part of why we call them "great." But we all know that there's also a dangerous busy-ness trap, which quickly becomes antithetical to a great work environment.

Our "work" has become so all-consuming that each day, nearly every great, or potentially great, person in the company gets "tapped out" in terms of time, energy, and resources. In places like the U.S., where workaholism is a quietly admired condition, we wear a constant state of exhaustion like a badge of honor in public, while simultaneously despising it in secret.

In most organizations, we are so busy "doing things" that we quickly lose all sense of space to tell if we're doing the *right* things. At the end of the day, there's no one left to actually focus ON the business itself. Even enormous companies, with swarms of HR people and a big learning and development staff who, it seems, *should* be entirely focused on making the business more work-conducive, don't seem to be able to actually execute these activities in real life.

Why is that?

Primarily, this isn't a behavior problem. It's a *structure* problem.

Think about the list of companies you've interacted with in your career. How many do you know that have even *one* person whose job it is to help make sure other people can do their work well? It's important to note that when I say "this is their job,"

I mean this is what they *get measured on*. During performance conversations, they are held accountable to *how well they've helped others in the company better use their strengths and become more engaged.*

In small organizations these people are almost non-existent. In these companies we haven't even given them a space. This is a structure problem.

In larger organizations these people might exist in title but are often completely neutered, paralyzed by bureaucracy and unable to truly pioneer any kind of lasting change. In these companies we haven't given them enough authority over internal systems. This is another structure problem.

This won't work in the new economy. *We have a missing link*—we are missing an organizational place for environment architects.

In business, we spend an exorbitant amount of time and attention on outcomes that don't predict *anything* (like finances), while the real drivers of human behavior (which happen to predict the finances) go almost completely ignored. Why do we spend hour after hour pouring over financials that indicate what happened *yesterday* instead of focusing on creating and sustaining the behaviors and work environment that will ensure better financials *tomorrow*? This usually isn't some kind of conspiracy or an exercise in misdirection, although it sometimes looks a little like both. Instead, it's mostly *ignorance*.

As mentioned in the *New Answers* section, most of us learn to work by watching role models. We work the way we do because it's the way we've seen other people work. It's tacit. An undercurrent. Our managers had bad meetings, so we have bad meetings. Our managers did our reviews one way, so we do it that way. Our managers treated "followers" like crap, so we do, too (even though we don't really mean to).

Our motivations are invisible—and *powerful*.

The power of our mindset, the effect of our working environment, the strength of our choices, the control of a company culture, the influence of what we believe to be true about the world—like the winds of a hurricane, these are all things that cannot be directly seen but can wreak havoc upon our physical world.

Or they can enhance it in a beautiful way.

There's nothing quite like a cool breeze on a warm summer evening.

Invisible things matter a great deal. But in most workplaces, there is simply no category for the type of person who can use their strengths and talents and gifts and intellect and training to truly *focus on the invisible.* There are very few people who are there explicitly to help make sure the organization is producing the right kind of ecosystem.

Some might think that these individuals would be "managers" or at the very least, the "Senior Leadership," but it doesn't really happen that way in practice. These people are generally stuck in meetings or too busy focusing on things like quarterly earnings and stock price.[109]

Others might think environment architects would be found in the HR or training department, but they don't really exist there, either. These folks may want to help build a great culture, but most are too busy defending the organization from internal troublemakers or they're buried in paperwork.

A tribe behaves badly for the exact same reason an individual does: we may "know" better, but we do it this way because it's always been done this way. We're not being intentionally blind, we're just ignorant to other possibilities. So we keep bringing in "change management" specialists who attempt to catalyze movement and growth. If they're successful at all, it is in small, localized pockets of individuals and teams.

But nothing *systemic* ever changes, does it?

Of course not... because it *can't*.

The systems we've built—the structures and policies and procedures and tools and everything else that makes up a work environment—are outdated. They are built to make sense of an industrial, destructive world that broke things into pieces and then rebuilt them in predictable and linear ways.

This is not the world that exists anymore.

I'm not suggesting that we stop making things or even ignore the progress made in the world over the past centuries. In fact, the cumulative nature of evolution won't allow us to un-do it, even if we wanted to. I *am* suggesting that we must progress *beyond* it—and that, in mindset, we already are.

Innovations that continually improve the way we "make stuff" are already killing "old world" jobs everywhere. This is not an American phenomenon, either—manufacturing jobs are disappearing all over the world.[110] Instead, this is just a natural way new technology continually pushes culture forward.

This viral spread of efficiency will continue to spread until manufacturing requires no humans at all. Though this day seems far off, it's closer than we think due to compounding innovations. It's important to recognize this as the eventual reality, because it helps us figure out what to do *today*.

If this is the direction technology is pushing us, then the opportunity lies in the science of how to unlock the creative capacity of human beings. We need to architect organizational environments that empower people to do more things that are clearly and decisively human. Our physical spaces must foster the kind of work that a machine, by its very definition, will *never* be able to do.

There are humans whose talents are perfectly aligned with making environments better and more life-giving—they are just currently scattered throughout many professions.

These people are landscape artists and industrial designers and urban planners. They are interior designers, human factors students, psychologists, and mood creators. They are UI/UX developers, curators, tailors, and artists.

They are interdisciplinary and creative folks who understand the impact their work has on the productivity/mood/joy/life of the people who experience it.

They know, and care, how their work impacts people. In fact, what motivates them is improving the quality of life of the people who interact with their "art" (for they do consider it that).

These are the individuals we're missing in our organizations. With every day that passes we feel the void of their gifts more strongly. In a world that is unquestionably dependent on finding ways to inspire, motivate, and enable the creative genius of people, we are utterly stalled without environment architects.

We've put the cart before the horse, however. Even if we could "get" them, there would be no place for them to "fit" in our current organizational model.

Where would they go?

HR?

R&D?

Sales?

There's no "department" even *remotely* appropriate for this utterly crucial component of talent.

This is why we need something new.

We must re-imagine what it means to organize an organization, and we must do it from an entirely new vantage point.

Tomorrow's economy is one based on collaboration and cooperation—fundamentally different from yesterday's model of coercion and competition.

If we're going to succeed, we have to start with the structure. And we need to create space in this structure for environment architects.

IGNITION POINT

How can we use these ideas to begin transforming the way we work? Answer the following questions to start a fire of your own:

What are a couple words or phrases I can consciously use more to construct a better world around me?

How do my perceptions change when I think about people's work as being about "architecting" (instead of "leading") and "building" (instead of "following")?

How much attention do I give the details of my work environment? What are three "small" things I can improve that would have a large impact?

How could my work environment be improved if we had someone whose job it was to focus on it? What would I fix first?

There's another problem with the industrial approach to building a work structure: an imbalance of talent. When we use people and their hands to help our businesses scale, we end up with a small group of people at the "top" (leaders) and a great majority at the "bottom" (followers).

Simply put, this is a reinforcement of the upside-down funnel communication method.

We've discussed this phenomenon, and suggested new terminology for these categories—Architects and Builders—that will help us equalize these two groups. But new words are just the beginning. We also need a new dominant metaphor for how we understand career paths inside a new kind of organization.

In most companies, even if it's not deliberately stated, there is a lurking old-world mindset implying that "leaders" and "followers"—with one at the "top" and one at the "bottom"—have different capabilities and that *one is more important than the other.*

As a result of this lingering mentality, which has been passed down through generation after generation, sometimes subconsciously and sometimes overtly, we end up with certain natural human abilities being completely undervalued and others being totally overvalued. [111]

We have a talent imbalance.

The thinkers and influencers and strategists—the Architects—get elevated *beyond* their worth.

The doers and creators and makers—the Builders— get demoted and minimized *below* their worth.

This isn't just wrong in human terms; it's also completely detrimental to organizational productivity in the emerging economy.

Here's a very simple way to understand why this hierarchical model of organizational design is fundamentally flawed. There's an area of study called "talent theory," which essentially states that humans all have different amounts of natural ability to do things, and that these abilities lie in different areas.[112]

In common parlance, this means I am naturally *good* at certain things and naturally *bad* at others, as are you.

This theory has been rigorously researched, and also seems to be fairly self-evident. If we accept this as being true, however, we must also accept that our current hierarchal method of organization is quite broken.

Why? Because it only allows one path "up."

People with all sorts of different natural abilities are crammed into this one-path model, which puts "builders" at the bottom and "architects" at the top.

I became acquainted with this conundrum firsthand when I finished my undergraduate degree. As many do, I left the university with grand plans and sweeping desires to leave my mark on humanity in a unique way.

I quickly discovered there was no place for me to do it.

My unique talents are predominantly in the Architect category, and entry-level architect positions simply *don't exist.*[113]

In today's organizations, the thinkers and strategists are found *only* on the "other side" of the builders. Much to my frustration, this meant that there was no real-life, practical way for me to do work which allowed me to a) be fulfilled at work or b) provide the most beneficial contribution I could make to the organization I worked with.

Wouldn't it be better if we could create organizations where individuals with all sorts of talents would be welcomed and mentored at all levels?

Where the structure of the organization itself fostered a mentality that we are all OK—no, that we are *BRILLIANT*—with the strengths we've got, instead of constantly being criticized for what we're missing?

Where we don't have to pretend to be (or pretend to *want* to be) a "manager" if we really *don't want to*?

Where we don't feel compelled to take a promotion we don't care about just to "climb the corporate ladder" or get a raise?

Wouldn't it be better to work in a place where success is redefined as an awareness of self and a mastery of one's craft? Wouldn't it make more sense for a career path to be a reflection of how much growth we can display through greater value creation for the tribe? Wouldn't it be nice if we could have a workplace that then encourages the usage of those abilities to help broader society?

We cannot do this with the way organizations are built now.

It's not structurally possible.

As things are today, we are wasting an *unthinkable* amount of latent human potential. The passion and creativity and innovation of our people lies dormant while individuals strive endlessly to get on a ladder they don't even care about.

Most times, outside of an occasional pang of discontent, we don't even notice that we're on a forever-spinning hamster wheel—the always-on systems we've built don't allow us to stop long enough to see it.

This model is outdated, nonsensical, and completely counterproductive.

We must stop thinking of our organizations as a pyramid, with only room for one at the peak.

What if, instead of a pyramid, our organizations were a **bridge**?

The architecture of a bridge allows for *many* supports that, when designed properly, all *reach the same height*—the height of the road. Depending on where these supports are located in the span, they may be built differently or serve slightly different purposes, but each pier (support column) works together to improve the stability and function of the bridge.

The road atop the bridge, in turn, allows connections to form between previously unreachable locations.

It helps people solve problems.

It makes society faster and more efficient.

It opens pathways for new kinds of trade.

It connects people that didn't know each other before.

Sometimes, a bridge even fixes issues people didn't even know they had.

Sounds like an organization with a world-changing product or service to me.

Building an organization like we are igniting an invisible tribe gives us an opportunity to completely re-imagine the way a group can be organized.

We have an emerging economy where we *need* to leverage the genius in every person. This means creating a separate "pier" for each category of job isn't just a happy thought—it is a necessity for success. We are entering a marketplace where the war for talent is insane, and only getting crazier. This means being able to create an organizational structure that provides pathways of mastery is another strategy that won't stay a "nice perk" for long, but will soon be imperative to retain the best people.

Is your organization a pyramid, with one path to the "top?" Or is your organization fostering a bridge mentality?

Only one of these models will help your organization survive the work revolution (and the pharaohs aren't going to like it).

DRAWING
BETTER
LINE$

When we think about building a bridge-like organizational structure where we deliberately have multiple pillars for many different kinds of workplace strengths, all of which support and reinforce the overall mission, we quickly recognize that we're going to have to begin measuring people very differently.

Of course, we measure all sorts of things now. Not surprisingly, however, most of today's calculations are measurements for the old world, not the new one.

Right now, we measure efficiency, production numbers, and variability. We measure failures and losses, and we measure revenues and profits. We have boatloads of competencies and "key performance indicators." These things are all relatively easy to quantify because they're based on a rational, predictable world.

Remember the *New Rules*, though: the emerging world doesn't see work from the linear perspective of a Scientist.

What would we measure if we were to see work like an Artist, instead?

We'd measure organizations, team members, and projects in terms of wholeness and creativity—in words like "meaning" and "impact."[114] We'd look for things like "value" and "emotional connection." We'd strive for continual development of strengths and a deeper sense of mastery. These things seem harder to quantify, because we're not used to thinking this way in a business context.[115]

When we look at our companies through this lens, we quickly realize that the majority of our companies are actually designed to minimize nonconformist, artistic behavior. Right now, *everything* is designed for us to color inside the old, outdated lines.

But what if we could draw new, *better* lines?

The things we measure are the things that actually matter. While this statement may seem to go in the "Duh, obvious!" category at first glance, this phenomenon goes much deeper than we initially think.

In our companies, we say we want our customer service folks to treat customers like gold, right? These kinds of behaviors keep customers coming back, encouraging them to spend more.[116]

However, the things we measure usually *counteract* this desire for outstanding service.

Most companies don't have "wowing customers" as a metric.[117] Instead, we measure our customer service representatives on how *little* time they can spend with customers. When we do this, no amount of "The Customer Comes First" rhetoric will **ever** overcome that measurement. It *can't*, because it's not what we're measuring. No matter how much we insist that's what we want, it can only ever be lip service. Our reps are forever confined to work within the limits of their lines.

This is how it works in every walk of life, by the way.

In sports, players play to the statistics defined for them.[118]

Companies adhere to environmental regulations set for them by the federal government.

Doctors conform to the best practices as defined by the professional organizations in their field.[119]

This has powerful implications for us as leaders, entrepreneurs, and change agents. It means we can help our tribe to think about our work in a more artistic way, but to do this *we must evaluate some very different things.*

We need new organizational rules: ones that measure things like an Artist, not like a Scientist.

Of course, when we talk about organizational rules, we don't travel very far before we run into compensation. After all, everyone needs to make money to survive. More than that, though, a healthy and honorable "trade" arises when someone exchanges their talents and abilities for something they need but can't procure efficiently on their own.

At a very basic level, a fair monetary exchange is what keeps a society balanced and functional.[120]

Our companies have a tremendous responsibility to honor this balance, and more importantly, to *elevate* the dialogue about money in the new economy.

In the world of the upside-down funnel, it was easy to disrespect this balance because the authority was inherently hierarchal. It is not this way anymore, and the flattening of power structures and communication will continue pushing our organizations towards greater transparency and fairness—particularly around our compensation models.

In order to get ahead of the curve and "ride the wave" on this issue, we should begin to see compensation and budgets as simply an extension of the overall organizational environment we design.

The truth is that our budgets are moral documents, declaring to the world in the most tangible way what our values really are.[121] Just like the environment we design and the things we measure, how we spend our money says *everything* about what we truly hold in high regard.

How we pay people is an important part of our company culture, but it isn't the real reason people work. We can see this clearly by how little money matters to people—when it's fair.[122] Once set, it becomes part of the invisible fabric that makes up the "institution."

Whether we're talking about compensation policies, the way we handle performance reviews, or how we run our meetings, each tribe has invisible measurements that define the social agreements of the organization. The "lines we draw" around how we are allowed to behave with each other are profoundly meaningful.

Before co-founding the Strengths Doctors consulting practice with me, my business partner Marvin Arnsdorff was a chiropractor for approximately twenty years. In workshops, Marvin will often make a peculiar statement: *"Structure determines function."* When explaining what he means, he shows that the "alignment" of a structure always determines the health of the larger unit.

In a human body, the alignment of the spine dictates how much mobility the person experiences.

In a car, the alignment of the tires determines how straight the vehicle drives.

In golf, proper alignment of the club with the ball sends the ball straight down the fairway.[123]

In a daily agenda, the alignment of proper discipline promotes greater freedom.

In an engine, the alignment of the pistons controls the output of energy.

Structure always determines function.

Our organizations are no different.

What kind of structure are you building?

In the first section, *New Answers*, we discussed the significance of rules in sports. The lines on the field or on a court are the same as the policies and systems we put in place in our companies. The lines we draw determine what we measure, which in turn determines what really matters in the tribe.

Furthermore, people just like you and me *made up* the rules our companies are now following. As much as we sometimes think they are, the rules we are following were **not** carved into a rock by GOD. If we want new lines, we can draw better ones.

In fact, I hear Architects are pretty good at this kind of thing.

IGNITION POINT

How can we use these ideas to begin transforming the way we work? Answer the following questions to start a fire of your own:

Is my organization structured like a pyramid or a bridge? How many pathways to mastery do I have where I work?

What would it be like to work in a place where I didn't feel like I had to climb a ladder designed for someone else in order to advance in my career? Visualize this experience; how does it make you feel?

What does my organization measure now? What do these measurements tell me about what we value, as a group?

What kind of things should we be measuring? (*Feel free to look back if you need a few suggestions!*)

FEWER ARMIES,
MORE
ORCHESTRAS

In most of the greatest cities of the world, usually somewhere near the center of town, there is a magnificent building. It might be very old or very new, but despite its age it is always a destination— because it is a place for people to gather and enjoy something magical:

Music.

Resounding in concert halls from every corner of the earth on a nightly basis, orchestras perform the greatest symphonies ever written for the throngs of people who come to do nothing but sit... and listen.

A professional musicians' life is completely absorbed with their instrument, whatever it may be. They practice intensely. They focus intently. They rehearse with abandon and play with passion, because they are obsessed with nothing but pure mastery of their craft.

For them, their work is art.

Concert musicians don't just play by themselves, of course—they play as part of the orchestra. Occasionally one instrument will have a featured solo, but even this is always woven into the larger whole. The music is a dance, a melodic—almost sacred—give and take, with notes and harmonies and silence and rhythm passing from one group of instruments to the next.

Their diligence as individuals and as a group is *our* reward as listeners, for nothing captivates the human soul quite like breathtaking music expertly performed.

What if *your* work could be art, too?

This is the business of the future we've been describing: an organic, artistic tribe where all parts are equally essential to the "music" being played. Where individual contributions are honored and essential, but also balanced with the mission of the whole tribe. Guiding the group is a conductor who doesn't lead from "on high" but from the bottom of the pit.

The new world is fundamentally different (creative versus destructive) and therefore, our organizations must be organized in a fundamentally new way.

In our work we need more mastery.

We need more *magic*.

In the old command and control model, we had managers at the "top" who would bark orders "down" to the makers.

We had "generals" and "soldiers."[124]

The problem is that the marketplace doesn't *need* scads of soldiers anymore.

What we *do* need are groups of people who are individually empowered to perform their work in a creative, interesting, masterful way.

We need fewer armies.

We need more orchestras.

DESIGNING AN ORGANIZATION THAT DOESN'T SUCK

Thankfully, there's a word—an **idea**—that gives us a starting point for designing a new kind of organization. It's what absolutely *everyone* in business wants, and it provides our fulcrum for a new kind of organization:

VALUE.

Not values. Value. (Singular.)

In the new economy, **value** is what runs the show. It's what absolutely *everyone* wants. Let me illustrate:

What does a customer want? Something of *value* from the company—a fair exchange for their money, time, or effort.

What does an employee want? For their work to be seen as something of *value*, and for their time and energy to be spent in a way that has *value*.

What does an owner want? To know their employees are working on projects that create *value* for the organization.

What does an organization (hopefully) want? For the tribe to create something of *value* for the larger society.

Absolutely *everything* pivots around the idea of value.

So, **value** is the perfect origin from which to build our new organizational framework.

Even more importantly, it helps us answer the deeper question of *"Why do we work?"*

Remember, we work because it is **valuable to *us*** (it uses our gifts/strengths) and because it's **valuable to *society*** (it makes the world better).

This kind of work is all but impossible in the type of organizations we have now.

In a value-centric company, however, it's not only possible, but the shape of the organization *actually pushes it further in that direction.*

When we come at organizational design from a value perspective, we start with one question:

"How do people create value for the tribe they work with?"

We first discussed this question in the *New Problems* section. Until each person in our organization can instantly answer the question "Why am I here?" with a sense of clarity and purpose, we will be stuck in the mindset of an old-world company.

It will be up to each of us as individuals to answer the question of *personal* purpose in our own unique flavor, taking into consideration our unique talents, our passions, and our life experiences.[125] But our organization can provide a safe place in which to do this by *building the proper structure.*

Here is the great opportunity for leaders, entrepreneurs, and change agents: to design an organization so it ignites an invisible tribe. To do this, we need a structure that:

- Allows people to be smart and agitated at work
- Connects deeply with the "some," not the "most"
- Builds sustainable processes (human and environment)
- Utilizes people's strengths, gifts, and talents
- Allows individuals to connect their passion to their work
- Reinforces a holistic and artistic mindset
- Creates a continual capacity for change
- Equalizes "Architects" and "Builders"
- Measures the things which truly create value

This seems like an awfully lofty task. But if we can accept that it is possible, *it will be.*

Together, *we can do this.*

There is a reason why this is one of the last chapters of the book and not the first. Finding research to support the benefits of a new kind of company isn't very difficult.[126] **Believing** we can create a new kind of organization, though—*that* is the hard part.

Hopefully by now you not only believe, you agree that there is no other reasonable way forward.

An organization that is life-giving instead of life-sucking—this is what we're after.

When we start with how people create value, we can get there.

Instead of structuring a company according to tasks or functions, which is how a Scientist would build a company for the old world, we design our tribe around *value*. This is a deliberate architectural choice. It is an Artist's answer to a new world where different things are scarce.

In this world, we start with **WHY**.

Why is a person here? *Why* are they part of this particular tribe?

"Why" questions, when answered honestly, always lead us to authentic **value**.

Try it.

Why are you here?

Because I help _____ .

Because I make _____ .

Because I improve _____ .

Because I build _____ .

Because I love _____ .

Each of us enters a tribe with our own unique motivations for being there; frankly, there are probably as many inspirations as there are people. But as a *group*, there are a finite number of ways for a tribe to create value.

Five ways, to be specific.

Throughout this book, we've discovered that our current departmental organizational structure is terribly broken.

Because it is based on breaking work into tasks, it is reductionistic in philosophy instead of being mosaic-minded. This makes a functional model too shortsighted in a world yearning for greater connection and sustainability.

When it comes to fostering creative and interesting work, a functional model doesn't scale well. It is limited in its capabilities to organize because it puts people into boxes that are too small to contain the breadth of their passions and talents.

A functional model can't provide the meaning that we yearn to find in our work, because it treats us like machines that only exist to perform specific activities.

We know we need something new. The five categories of value can be that new structure.

I call these categories **Value Groups,** and they are:

1) Creative

2) Community

3) Culture

4) Currency

5) Conductor

We can think of these as the five C's of value creation, and they can help us design a completely new kind of organization—one that doesn't suck, and in fact does the opposite.

Right now, we have "departments" in our companies. These groups exist because all the people in it "do" similar things. But as we travel further into the new kind of economy described throughout this book, the value of a job will be found less in its *function* and more in *how each person's talents create value for the group.*[127]

Structurally, we leverage this transition by re-organizing our organizations from departments into Value Groups, which correspond with the five categories of how teams can create value.

At the macro level of a new-world organization (tribe), these five groups should exist:

CREATIVE

The Creative group creates value by building a remarkable product that is efficiently and sustainably produced. These people are found in the former departments of manufacturing and engineering, and on the factory floor. They are code developers and graphic designers. They are the people who love turning ideas into something real and tangible.

These people make stuff. *Great* stuff.

COMMUNITY

The Community group creates value by building a tribe of brand ambassadors around the company's products or services. They develop relationships. These people used to be referred to as "salespeople." To work in the emerging economy, they will need to become more about wowing customers and fostering an ongoing conversation than anything else.

These people connect customers to something that makes their lives better.

CULTURE

The Culture group creates value by ensuring the organization has a healthy and vibrant culture which appreciates, energizes, and develops its people. As we've discussed, this group will be an entirely new construct in tomorrow's organization. They are the mash-up of designer, landscape artist, and curator discussed in *God Is In The Details.*

These people cultivate and grow a healthy work environment.

CURRENCY

The Currency group creates value by managing the flow of money to the internal team (employees) and the external constituents (vendors). Everyone from the CFO to all accountants and payroll people fit here. They help find and provide the resources to fund great projects. These people are numbers and data people (they love them).

These people use figures and funds to help make great things happen.

CONDUCTOR

This person was formerly known as the CEO. They used to sit at the "top" of the upside-down funnel and look down upon loyal (or not-so-loyal) subjects. No longer. The power has flattened and they now look *up* into the organization. Their primary job is talent liberation, enabling every individual to realize their potential. The Conductor creates value by helping the other 4 C's work "in concert."

This is the "big cheese" who realizes he or she is now leading from the "bottom of the pit," like an orchestra conductor.

It should also be noted that within these groups, two are predominantly comprised of Architects and two are primarily made of Builders.

The Creative and Community groups are typically Builders. They **build** great products and great relationships, respectively.

The Culture and Currency groups are usually Architects. They **design** great places to work and the rules for how money flows, respectively.

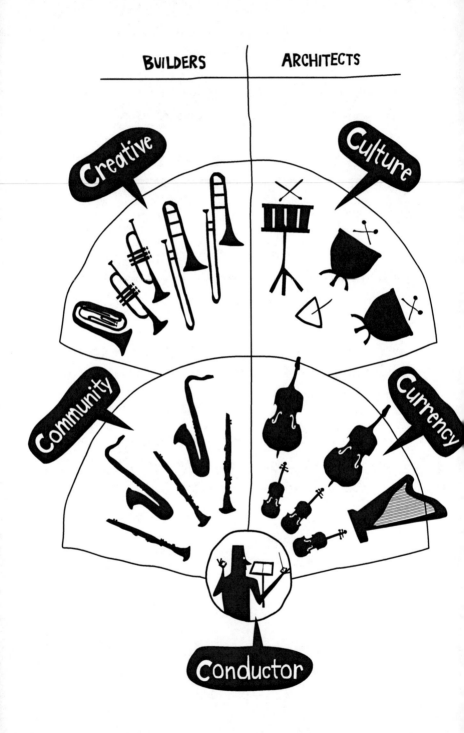

By reorganizing in this way, it is ensured that every individual in the company is provided a very clear structure for how they create value for the organization. When a person is hired, they are not hired for a "position" as much as they are hired "into a Group."

In this world, the question "What Group are you in?" becomes more self-identifying than an individual title.

The very language we use in a value-centric model reinforces the power of collaboration and teamwork ("I am not alone, but part of a larger 'group'"). It also continually reminds each person exactly how his or her strengths and talents best create value for the larger tribe ("As a member of the Community Group, I am a relationship builder.").

This model also provides a clear framework for how a company might be "physically" reorganized.

There will always be paradoxical tension between "Me" and "We," but this model puts both in their rightful place.

Furthermore, in this structure "value" can become nearly synonymous with "passion." By building Value Groups, we allow people to self-select into the category they are most passionate about—groups that by their very nature describe how they create value for the larger group. This one step, in itself, boosts employee engagement, at both an individual and team level.

How?

We all have certain activities which energize us, and these things vary from person to person. Most organizations can't take advantage of this because their org chart is designed around tasks and functions. Leaders can "encourage" their people to *try* to find ways to do activities they enjoy in their current jobs, but they are effectively paralyzed in their ability to *create the structural space* necessary to leverage that energy.

But when we redesign the structure in a value-centric way (at a team or whole-company level), we simply use our knowledge about people's unique passions to help them find their way into the right Value Group!

Interestingly, but not surprisingly, what people are most passionate about often lines up exactly with how they create the most value for the organization. We just need to get them into that place—and now we know how.

When we do this, we get a tremendous win-win-win-win (I know it seems dramatic, but it truly is four wins):

1) The **customers and vendors** win because they get to interact with people who love their work.

2) The **employees** win because they get to do things at work that energize them.

3) The **company owners** win because people who are passionate about what they're doing on the job do *much* better work.

4) The **society at large** wins because the organization is more likely to produce something that actually makes the world better.

At first, creating Value Groups may feel like creating departments. Are we simply grouping people into new silos with cooler, more-alliterated names?

The difference, which seems small but means everything, is the *motivation*.[128] The reason departments exist now is mostly because of tradition—although part of it is convenience, and a little bit is laziness. We grouped people who performed certain tasks and functions together because in a mechanical and predictable world, it made sense to do so. Departments were the in-office equivalent of the sections of an assembly line—each one a new stop on a linear path to the goal.

As discussed, however, work has become more creative and complex and the effectiveness of this model has been steadily breaking down. Now, individual job descriptions feel fuzzy and interdepartmental communication is essential. What we "do" is infinitely more nuanced than it used to be, and performing really great work requires a holistic understanding of the company's product or service. This causes workers to often feel like an organic appendage artificially attached to a robotic process—told to be more human and yet act like a machine. We've become so disconnected from the original intention of our organization that we've lost any sense of purpose.

Value Groups "fix" the above problems at the motivation level. They provide an architecture flexible enough to embed continual change into the fabric of the organization and they continually reinforce the "big picture" of why the tribe exists. They encourage each person to bring their most imaginative and interesting ideas to the team and they equalize the different kinds of work. They foster autonomy and help people work on projects they care deeply about.

Essentially, they leverage the power of invisible tribes.

They are the structural solution to a problem we've felt for many years, but have just been patching with proverbial band-aids.

I also wish to address the "silo" conundrum—a serious issue in a department-centric organization. By their very nature, being part of a Value Group is a broader notion than having a position within a department. There can only be four groups, after all (outside the Conductor), meaning the affiliation of the group is much more "loose" by design.

Within this flexible container, there are all sorts of organizational models that allow for über-efficient communication and teamwork.[129]

Furthermore, this structure "forces" (in a benevolent way) each person to be *crystal* clear on his or her individual value proposition.[130] People in a value-centric organization do not have a "job," they have a personal brand which is driven by their unique strengths. Also, work in this kind of structure is intentionally project-driven, so each person will naturally have to form teams requiring complementary strengths. Many of these team members will likely be found in other Groups, thereby naturally preventing silos from even forming at all.

From a belonging and value-creation standpoint, Value Groups help each person feel like they are part of something bigger than themselves, while continually providing clarity around how they can use their talents to create value for the larger group.

Because it is more of a loose connection than a department, a Value Group also differs in its leadership. Where a department might have a "Department Head," "VP," or "Manager," a Value Group does not. Instead, a Value Group may have a Lead Architect—but as you can tell from the title, what this person would actually *do* would be light years apart from today's "manager." Right now we have managers who attempt to "manage" things, but an architect would be focused on designing opportunities for people in the group to better know and collaborate with each other.

Even more likely, project teams would just form and disband regularly inside this larger structure, with an appropriate Project Lead assigned to help coordinate whatever the current initiative is.

It should be said that Value Groups aren't intended to be the "be all, end all" solution of organization design, foreverandeveramen.

They are simply the next development in our organizational evolution.

It's time to take that step.

IGNITION POINT

How can we use these ideas to begin transforming the way we work? Answer the following questions to start a fire of your own:

If my organization were an orchestra, would we be making beautiful music that people would come to watch?

How often do my organization's leaders talk about creating value?

How often do *I* talk about creating value? How can I make this a bigger part of the way I speak?

Do I know how I best create value for my organization? Distill it into one sentence and put it here:

How often do I, or others in my organization ask "Why?" Is questioning our processes and procedures an acceptable practice? What are examples of systems in my culture that make me wonder, "Why do we do it this way?"

If I were to pick one of the five Value Groups to belong to, which would it be?

For too long, we have been neglecting a very necessary organizational evolution. In the new world, we simply cannot afford to continue pushing people to be more human at work while at the same time providing them workplaces that are anything but.

We need organizations that are life-giving instead of life-sucking.

When we understand that the world is growing more holistic, collaborative, and creative and we begin to see how a business can leverage this mindset, we are able to predict some really exciting things for the future.

We can see visions for a much better way to work.

Specifically, we can envision organizations that are finally able to truly leverage the unique gifts/talents/ strengths of individuals because they are finally able to capitalize on a truly collaborative business atmosphere.

In a world where we had to be all things to all people, we could never truly hone in on our specific areas of mastery. That world is gone. Now we can specialize in a way we've never been able to before. But this specialization must be balanced with an understanding of integration. Like the pieces of a mosaic which only make sense in the context of the whole image, our specialized skills will only add value when they are an integrated part of the larger tribe's mission.

From this, there are two realizations:

1) It will be our ability to respect each individual's uniqueness that will make this new world thrive, and

2) As we march further down this road, the human family will grow even more interconnected and interdependent.

There is a "Me" and a "We," and we desperately need them **both** to thrive in the new world.

The business that blooms in the emerging economy is led by people who understand that business isn't about control, but about *connection*.

It's about connecting people to each other.

It's about connecting businesses to their customers.

It's about connecting organizations to the needs of larger society.

A tribe is the basic human grouping which creates connection points. Everything about the way the world is changing suggests that our viability as a leader, entrepreneur, change agent, or organization will be determined by our ability to leverage the power of the connections both inside and between tribes.

The organizations that will thrive in this ecosystem are the ones who can build a value-centric mesh of communication which can not only bend and flex and grow but also provide enough of a framework for people to feel secure and connected. The people who will succeed will be the Architects who design life-giving work environments and the Builders who create remark-able products and customer service that makes people exclaim: "*Wow!*"

The company that succeeds tomorrow looks almost nothing like the business of today. It is an organization made up *of* people, lovingly designed *by* people, and run *for* the wellbeing of all people.

So… what future are **you** creating?

The world is fundamentally reorganizing itself around wholeness and meaning. We are shifting towards a holistic philosophy that values the "big picture" impact of our lives.

More than ever before in all of human history, it's now becoming possible to find and gather the people who align with a specific mission. But these groups have a tremendous amount of autonomy, which means this new opportunity brings an inherent challenge: *while these people may be easily found, they will not be motivated with old rules.*

Never before in the history of the world have we been able to organize at this scale around the things that actually interest people.

There are invisible tribes all around you. And they are ready to **GO**.

They are just waiting for someone—*YOU!*—to tap into their power.

They are communities of passion; groups of people who desperately want to band together to support your cause, your endeavor, and your dream. *They just need someone to organize them in a way that liberates their abilities to work toward a common goal.*

Will you be the courageous individual who ignites an invisible tribe?

I hope you will. The world needs you.

Together, we can create something better than what we've had. We can design an organization that doesn't suck.

What are **you** *going to do?*

IGNITION POINT

How can we use these ideas to begin transforming the way we work? Answer the following questions to start a fire of your own:

What am I going to do differently now?

ACKNOWLEDGEMENTS

My most sincere thanks to:

Jim Seybert for reading this book about a bazillion times through about two-bazillion iterations; whatever this is, it wouldn't be half as good without your input.

Frank Breeden for your invaluable insight.

Stephanie Storey for that lunch at Alcove, and for reading the whole thing again after I re-wrote it.

Jason Walton for seriously getting in my head and spitting out so many kick-ass illustrations.

Al Restivo for teaching me about the power of focus.

William Now for the epic phone calls.

Joseph Michelli, Terry Paulson, Carleen MacKay, and Dave Logan for so kindly endorsing this project early on.

Austyn, Nick, and Jeannie at Silver Thread, for your patience with my detail orientation and incessant new ideas.

All my MBA Cohort 9 classmates; you have influenced me much more than you realize.

All my teachers and mentors at UNL/Gallup, especially Mike Morrison and Cheryl Beamer.

All the spectacular authors and thinkers I reference throughout this book; if I've come up with anything unique, it's only because I stand on your shoulders.

My partners in crime—I mean, business: Marvin, Greg, and Mike.

Will Gray for always entertaining a thoughtful discussion about the state of the world.

Mom, Dad, Dacia, Carol, Gordon, and Garrett for putting up with me going on about "writing a book" for year after year after year...

Allison. You are my favorite.

STRENGTHS DOCTORS

Strengths Doctors helps leaders and entrepreneurs build healthier organizations through a focus on strengths, engagement, and culture. We love meeting new people just like you. Send us a message!

www.strengthsdoctors.com

THE WORK REVOLUTION

The Work Revolution is a growing tribe of passionate rebels who are re-imagining and re-inventing the way business is done in order to make work meaningful for everyone. Join us!

www.workrevolution.org

ENDNOTES

1 The ways in which the world is changing makes ignorance a much flimsier excuse than it used to be, however. No longer are we "informationally" relegated to our social circles, the people in our immediate geographic area, or to a large degree, even our class or income level. The democratization of information via technology is putting excellence in the hands of almost anyone who wishes to find it. In other words: we will no longer be excused by the answer: "I just didn't know."

2 For more on this, read *You Have The Power To Choose Prosperity* by Umair Haque on the HBR blog. http://bit.ly/choose-prosperity

3 Download the Deloitte 2011 Shift Index. http://bit.ly/deloitte-shift-index-2011

4 Watch a video of me talking about this idea online. http://bit.ly/jad-passion-video

5 Read *Wellbeing* by Tom Rath & Jim Harter. http://wbfinder.com/

6 At the time of this writing, Apple, Inc. had more than $100 billion in cash reserves. This is more than the total operating cash balance of the United States. http://bit.ly/apple-100-billion

7 Watch a video of me talking about this idea online. http://bit.ly/jad-listen-video

8 If you're curious, http://icechewing.com/ and http://mlhh. org/ are legit. Although, if a graphic novel about a genetically modified porpoise exists, I'm sure it has a group somewhere, too.

9 There is also a danger inherent in this unconscious gathering. In science, it's called "confirmation bias," and it means that we naturally look to find information that confirms the things we already believe. The risk is that we can insulate ourselves within our niche group to the point where we hear no conflicting viewpoints. Sites like Google don't help with this either, as they "learn" our search patterns and begin to filter our results accordingly. For more on this large potential problem, watch Eli Pariser's TED talk *Beware Online 'Filter Bubbles.'* http:// bit.ly/filter-bubbles For an insightful short read on the topic, download article called *Cold-Filtered Collaboration* from Mike Prokopeak. http://bit.ly/cold-filtered

10 Watch a video of me talking about this idea online. http://bit. ly/jad-invisible-tribes-video

11 We're seeing the very beginning of the potential power of an invisible tribe with groups like Occupy Wall Street. It's incredible to imagine what a group like this could accomplish if they had a clear tribe leader. http://occupywallst.org/

12 In 2007 a study by ICM indicated that people waste 60 million hours every year on hold on customer "service" lines. http://bit.ly/60million-on-phone-hold

13 Read *Get Rid Of The Performance Review* by Samuel A. Culbert with Lawrence Rout. http://performancepreview.com/

14 Read *Why Excellence Is Not The Opposite Of Failure*, an excerpt from *First, Break All The Rules* by Marcus Buckingham and Curt Coffman. http://bit.ly/excellence-v-failure

15 Read *The Presentation Secrets of Steve Jobs* by Carmine Gallo. http://bit.ly/presentation-steve-jobs

16 Credit for the elegant dichotomy of "me" and "we" goes to my friend and mentor Mike Morrison. I'm fairly certain Mike's thinking has shaped mine in more ways than I even realize. http://learnplando.com

17 Some research seems to indicate that our actions are practically dictated by these invisible forces of habit and belief. Check out *The Power Of Habit* by Charles Duhigg. http://bit.ly/duhigg-habit

18 In our tribes/organizations/businesses the power of the invisible world is just as dramatic: 80% of a company's market value is due to completely invisible things. The productivity of our companies is primarily formed by intangibles like culture, morale, talent, a strong brand, meaning, and engagement. More on this in *Human Sigma* by John H. Fleming and Jim Asplund. http://bit.ly/gallup-human-sigma

19 Just in case you haven't noticed, I'm using the words "business," "organization," "tribe," and "company" fairly synonymously. As mentioned in the *New Rules* intro, whenever humans organize themselves into a group, there are similar patterns of action that occur. The theories presented in this book will help create healthier patterns of action and can be applied to any group that comes together for a common purpose.

20 Watch a video of me talking about this idea online. http://bit.ly/jad-coin-video

21 These shifts have been, and continue to be, brilliantly written about and explored by many hyper-intelligent individuals. A few I'd highly recommend checking out include Seth Godin (*Tribes, Linchpin,* etc.), Dan Pink (*Drive, A Whole New Mind*), Umair Haque (*The New Capitalist Manifesto*), Gallup Press (*Strengths Based Leadership, Human Sigma,* etc.), Dave Logan, John King, & Halee Fischer-Wright (*Tribal Leadership*), David Strauss & Neil Howe (*The Fourth Turning*), Clay Shirky (*Here Comes Everybody*), and Thomas Friedman (*The World Is Flat*).

22 A few examples: TED (http://ted.com), Khan Academy (http://khanacademy.org/), and Skillshare (http://skillshare.com).

23 For a long time, the business models of the entertainment industry were based on selling a physical product (CD's DVD's, etc.). At the core, however, most entertainment is not a physical "thing" at all, but a story, an idea, or a piece of information. As these things get translated into their digital equivalents, it is eviscerating the old world's entertainment business models. This will not stop, and it will not slow down.

24 I would include "currency" in the category of now-abundant resources, as well. Read *Idle Funds are the Devil's Playground* by Chris Meyer & Julia Kirby. http://bit.ly/idle-funds

25 *Why the End of Scarcity Will Change the Economics of Everything* by James L. McQuivey http://bit.ly/end-of-scarcity

26 *Abundance: The Future Is Better Than You Think* by Peter H. Diamandis and Steven Kotler. http://abundancethebook.com/

27 Watch a video called *Rethinking The Idea Of The Brand* by Umair Haque. http://bit.ly/rethinking-brand

28 For more on this, check out some articles from the Conscious Capitalism organization. http://bit.ly/conscious-brands

29 Read almost any article in the Gallup Business Journal for great research on this topic. http://businessjournal.gallup.com

30 If you are looking for more ideas to try, check out the MIX (Management Innovation eXchange). http://managementexchange.com

31 At the time of writing, Lady Gaga and Justin Bieber each have over *25 million* followers on Twitter (http://bit.ly/twitter-top100). Outside of the top twenty, not even the most watched TV series finales in history can claim this many people paying attention (http://bit.ly/most-watched-tv).

32 They never really have, honestly. It just didn't use to matter because scarcity of access to eyeballs via a very limited number of communication channels bottlenecked the scarcity at the content providers. It was a perfect business model... that is now unceremoniously dying. http://bit.ly/godin-music-lessons

33 We also have to care about the "some" much more than we used to. The new game is about quality over quantity.

34 From Robert Kiyosaki's *The Conspiracy of the Rich*. http://conspiracyoftherich.com/

35 Whether you believe this is happening or not, please go along with the example for a moment.

36 As I was writing this, Hurricane Irene was storming towards the East Coast, disrupting tens of millions of people.

37 For a recent, but classic, example, research the music industry. Download my eBook *The Sad Song of the Music Industry* for free. http://bit.ly/jad-sad-song

38 I'm tempted to make a few comments here about the homogenized, industrial education system that creates these kinds of people, but will save that for another book. If you want more right now, go visit http://uncollege.org.

39 For practical ideas on why and how to break an organization out of these kinds of chains, read *The Work Revolution: Freedom and Excellence For All* by Julie Clow. http://theworkrevolutionbook.com/

40 Then we yank it back out and pretend we've been thinking about it all along. This is ridiculous; isn't it time for something new?

41 Reference Dan Pink's *A Whole New Mind*. http://danpink.com/whole-new-mind

42 The shift out of a function-driven world is a transition that we are currently in the middle of, and it is not finished yet. As such, we see "pieces" of a kind of "industrial diaspora" occurring in fits and starts across the global economic landscape. Even in this time of rapid evolution, however, the marketplace is already placing a greater value and economic demand on activities that only humans at their most creative and imaginative can do.

43 Reference employee engagement reports by Gallup (http://bit.ly/gallup-engagement), Towers Watson (http://bit.ly/tw-engagement), and BlessingWhite (http://bit.ly/bw-engagement).

44 Credit goes to Seth Godin for initially asking the original derivative of these questions in his blog post *"Form and Function"* from October 24, 2011. http://bit.ly/form-and-function

45 You may say that humans in other countries still perform this kind of work, and you'd be right. But even this is diminishing. http://bit.ly/foxconn-robots

46 Innovation has always been this way: we create new technology (like email) which displaces old methods (like the post office)—even though every time we act as though we've never seen this phenomenon before. The speed of innovations is just compounded now, which gives us the impression (and maybe reality) of nearly incessant change.

47 Most of our financial system is set up to encourage confusion around this, which also doesn't help.

48 Not that these two new questions are easy to answer. They're not. "Simple" and "easy" are completely different things. http://bit.ly/the-good-simple

49 We may initially balk at the topic of "love" in a business-focused book. But you know as well as I do that if someone "loves their work" they do a much better job at it. In many ways, it really is that simple.

50 This elegant description is based on ideas I heard presented by Tim Keller. He, in turn, credits much of the basis for his ideas to Dorothy Sayers. They are both phenomenally prescient thinkers and communicators. If you are open to a spiritual perspective on the topic of work, I recommend reading *Why Work?* (http://bit.ly/sayers-why-work) by Ms. Sayers and listening to the talk simply entitled *Work* by Dr. Keller (http://bit.ly/keller-work).

51 For just a couple recommendations, check out *Life After College* by Jenny Blake (http://bit.ly/jenny-lac-book) and *Go Put Your Strengths To Work* by Marcus Buckingham (http://bit.ly/marcus-go-book).

52 Watch Simon Sinek's TEDx talk *How Great Leaders Inspire Action.* http://bit.ly/TED-start-with-why

53 If you're interested, they even compiled this list into a delightful little bedtime read called the DSM-IV.

54 We've known this for quite a long time, actually. http://bit.ly/rutherford-model

55 Read the short feature *Designer Babies* by Erin Biba from the August 2010 issue of Wired Magazine. http://bit.ly/designer-babies

56 Please watch *Waiting For 'Superman'* if you haven't. http://waitingforsuperman.com

57 *Watch Did You Know 3.0* on YouTube. http://bit.ly/did-you-know-2009

58 Read more about this in Malcolm Gladwell's *The Tipping Point*. http://gladwell.com/pdf/tipping.pdf

59 Read more about this in Marcus Buckingham and Curt Coffman's book *First, Break All The Rules.* There's also an excerpt on my blog. http://bit.ly/excellence-v-failure

60 Read *Many Paths To Engagement* by Jennifer Robison. http://bit.ly/paths-to-engagement

61 Read more about this in Daniel Pink's book *A Whole New Mind*. http://danpink.com/whole-new-mind

62 For an excellent treatise on the importance of meaning at work, read *Meaning, Inc.* by Gurnek Bains. http://bit.ly/meaning-inc

63 Coming full-circle to the age-old system of bartering (http://barterquest.com) ensures fair value is clearly understood and received by both parties, and it is experiencing a resurgence in popularity. http://bit.ly/bartering-new-economy Even "regular" banks are becoming more cooperative and holistic. http://bit.ly/cooperative-banking

64 Within my own spiritual tradition, a movement called Emergent has sprung up within the past few decades. http://emergentvillage.com/

65 Watch Martin Seligman's TED talk *The New Era Of Positive Psychology.* http://bit.ly/seligman-TED

66 Watch a video of me talking about this idea online. http://bit.ly/jad-scientist-artist-video

67 Though I've been thinking about this transition for a long time, these descriptions are another amazing bit of clarity I owe to Tim Keller. http://bit.ly/keller-work

68 Even though we're focused on organizational implications in this book, it's important to note the enormity and totality of how this shift affects *everything*. The insights discovered by studying a mosaic mindset can be cross-applied to many (if not all) areas of our lives.

69 A real story about a delightful woman named Sandy Greenawalt in Pennsylvania. http://bit.ly/tollbooth-oprah

70 Read Gary Hamel's amazing case study about Morning Star from the December 2011 issue of the Harvard Business Review. http://bit.ly/hamel-fire-managers

71 If you're curious why I used "eighty years" as my measurement, read *The Fourth Turning* by Neil Howe and David Strauss. http://bit.ly/fourth-turning

72 Art we call "timeless" has simply found a way to connect with enduring aspects of humanity (e.g. the human form in sculptures or paintings, falling in love and songs about the experience, etc.). Good art doesn't have to be about these timeless things—but if it's not, it's tied to a specific time.

73 Look at Moore's Law in technology, for example. http://bit.ly/moores-law-wiki

74 Gregg Easterbrook does a great job of articulating the implications of this choice in his book *Sonic Boom*. http://bit.ly/sonic-boom-book

75 Read Robert Safian's article *This Is Generation Flux: Meet The Pioneers Of The New (And Chaotic) Frontier Of Business* from the February 2012 issue of Fast Company. http://bit.ly/wired-generation-flux

76 For a bit more science here, check out the detailed response on the other side of this link. http://bit.ly/dying-cells

77 For more, read Seth Godin's seminal book *Tribes*. http://bit.ly/ godin-tribes-book

78 This is one reason why Gen Y'ers can drive people from other generations crazy. Older generations just aren't used to the constant disruption these early adopters are.

79 Recently, this idea has been all the rage amongst food providers, including Dunkin' Donuts, Mountain Dew, and Papa Johns. http://bit.ly/papajohns-facebook

80 A few I'd recommend checking out are Get Satisfaction (http://getsatisfaction.com) and Workface (http://workface. com).

81 Clearly much has been written about what made Toyota's methods so unique, but for a short introduction, visit their website (http://bit.ly/toyota-production-system). You can also watch a video about Toyota's joint partnership with GM in the 1980's at a plant in northern California called NUMMI (http://bit.ly/nummi-pt1). Outside of the auto industry, the idea of continual change and improvement can be found in the philosophy of kaizen and throughout the writings of some of the most popular organizational and management theorists of the last century, including Peter Senge and Peter Drucker. Clearly the concept of building an ethos of change into one's organization is not new. The ways in which the world is changing, however, are making this mindset a business imperative instead of a competitive advantage.

82 Check out Podio (http://podio.com), Rypple (http://rypple.com), Diaspora (http://joindiaspora.com), Asana (http://asana.com), and WorkSimple (http://getworksimple.com).

83 For more on the continual battle for organizational excellence, read anything by Jim Collins and his team.

84 Unless they have enormous storehouses of resources, as many multinational corporations do. Many of these institutions will ferociously resist the future and instead lobby for the past, only to be eventually and unceremoniously upended like the music industry. Progress can be slowed, but never stopped.

85 "Mission statements" don't have much impact because they usually don't get embedded in a culture—they just get pasted into a website or painted on a wall. A better way to look at this is from the book *Tribal Leadership* by Dave Logan, John King, and Halee Fischer-Wright. Here, the authors describe the driving force of a tribe as a "noble cause" and the values that support it. This is a much more feasible way to embed a sense of real mission into a culture. http://triballeadership.net/

86 At the time of writing, Facebook had just purchased Instagram for $1 billion and the Facebook IPO was occurring. History will tell how the Facebook story unfolds, but as of now the company is worth more than $100 billion dollars. Not bad for an eight-year old organization. http://bit.ly/facebook-worth

87 Polly LaBarre, in her article *How To Lead A Rich Life* which appeared in Fast Company in March 2003, noted: "The United States spends more on trash bags than ninety other countries spend on everything. In other words, the receptacles of our waste cost more than all of the goods consumed by nearly half of the worlds nations." We know this absurd imbalance doesn't feel right, but nothing will really change until we build our systems to appreciate connectedness. http://bit.ly/polly-rich-life

88 Please watch Annie Leonard's video called *The Story of Stuff.* http://bit.ly/story-of-stuff-vid

89 Check out this amazing visualization of these connections, created by an intern on Facebook's engineering team. http://bit.ly/facebook-visualization

90 Here's a press release from the Seattle Aquarium congratulating Pike Place on this remarkable achievement. http://bit.ly/pike-place-sustainable

91 Here's a bit more information on what the "seventh generation" idea is all about. http://bit.ly/seventh-generation

92 For more on this, read Mihály Csíkszentmihályi's work around the concept of "flow." http://bit.ly/flow-wiki

93 They have a real throne. For real. http://bit.ly/zappos-throne

94 Read Gary Hamel's wonderful case study on Morning Star online or in the December 2011 issue of the Harvard Business Review. http://bit.ly/first-fire-managers

95 60 Minutes did a segment on SAS awhile back, and you can watch it on YouTube (http://bit.ly/sas-vid-pt1). If you'd rather read about the magical place that is SAS, you can do that, too (http://bit.ly/cbs-sas-good-life).

96 Read more about the importance of rhythm in *Be Excellent at Anything: The Four Keys To Transforming the Way We Work* and Live by Tony Schwartz, Jean Gomes, and Catherine McCarthy. http://bit.ly/energy-book

97 There's even a dating site for Apple fanatics. Seriously. http://cupidtino.com/

98 Read more about the TOMS movement on their website. http://bit.ly/toms-movement Full disclosure: my company, Strengths Doctors, is a proud TOMS copycat. We love the one-for-one movement so much that we are committed to pioneering a one-for-one model in the service sector. http://bit.ly/give-1

99 For more on what makes Semco tick, read Polly LaBarre's article *What Does Fulfillment At Work Really Look Like?* on CNNMoney. http://bit.ly/semco-fulfillment

100 There's more background on this story in *Fellowship of the Ringlets* by Rachel Gross from the June 2012 issue of Wired Magazine. http://bit.ly/pixar-red-hair

101 Leonard Teo talks about the lengthy creation process of *Avatar* in an article for TechRadar. http://bit.ly/making-avatar

102 Learn more about the Integral Institute online. http://integralinstitute.org/

103 Watch a video of me talking about this idea online. http://bit.ly/jad-language-video

104 For a beautiful articulation of this, read *Stories Create The World* by Jeff Wise. http://bit.ly/stories-create-the-world

105 Will there be individuals within these categories that create more value than others, and therefore demand more compensation? Yes. People vary widely in their capacity for value creation, and therefore their ability to demand different value exchange is varied, as well. But the categories are equal.

106 I first read this phrase in a book by Stephen Sondheim called *Finishing The Hat*, although the quote doesn't seem to originate with him. http://bit.ly/God-in-detail

107 Read *Wellbeing* by Tom Rath and Jim Harter. http://bit.ly/
wellbeing-book

108 And please, for the love of all the leadership books in the world,
don't guess. Just ask your people, and don't pretend you
already know. You'll be surprised, I promise. Shameless plug:
My company, Strengths Doctors, would love to help you ask
the right questions to get the information you need to build a
healthier work environment. http://strengthsdoctors.com

109 Again, I am not blaming managers; this is something mostly
outside of their direct control. Sure, somewhere there is a
group of people making the rules around quarterly earnings
and financial reports, but most managers are not those
people. This means we've got another problem where the
core issue isn't behavior, but a structure that reinforces
unhealthy behavior.

110 One more reference to *Sonic Boom* by Gregg Easterbrook.
http://bit.ly/sonic-boom-book

111 When we examine income disparity rates, we're not talking
about "slightly more important," either. As reported by
Mother Jones from 2010 data, "the top one-hundredth of one
percent... now make an average of $27 million per household.
The average income for the bottom 90 percent...? $31,244."
http://bit.ly/income-inequality-mj

112 This idea also applies to organizations as a whole and entire nations, as well. For more on this, listen to Daniel Pink's interview with Marcus Buckingham on his *Office Hours* program (http://danpink.com/office-hours) or read some of David Ricardo's work around comparative advantage (http://bit.ly/comp-adv).

113 I will admit that I stumbled my way into a few exceptions. One way to get around this challenge is to work for a small enough company where it's possible to "rise" quickly into the leadership team. In this situation, talents for strategy and big-picture thinking are more valued (because there are fewer options), but most organizations still aren't overly welcoming to the 23-year-old strategist. If you want to explore why most groups can't do this (and I really do mean "can't," not "won't"), read about "Stage Three" tribes in the already-mentioned book *Tribal Leadership*.

114 At first glance, this may sound strange and über non-business-y. But it may help to know that the lead designer of the most valuable company in the world—at the time of this writing, Apple, Inc.—talks like this. http://bit.ly/ive-interview.

115 Interesting how the "soft" skills are always "harder" to master, isn't it?

116 Engaged customers spend WAY more money, by the way.

More on this in the already-mentioned-a-few-times book *Human Sigma.* http://bit.ly/gallup-human-sigma.

117 Zappos.com is an example of a company that does measure "wow." One could probably use that same word to describe their customer engagement levels. Coincidence? Nope.

118 For more on this read Andy Stefanovich's book *Look At More.* http://bit.ly/look-at-more

119 For more on this read Jennifer Robison's article *The Other $700 Billion Question.* http://bit.ly/other-700-billion

120 Sadly, many of today's measurements have been constructed for the benefit of the small groups at the top of the upside-down funnel, and as such they take advantage of large groups of other people (it's a 1% vs. 99% situation). Because of this, our society feels imbalanced; our core belief in "a fair trade" has been disrespected. At a human level, most of us believe there should be some consistency in the returns gained from giving our time and work abilities in exchange for the ability to pay our rent. Right now, this very basic social agreement feels bypassed. These are the very types of things that help ignite revolutions.

121 I did not invent the "budgets are moral documents" phrase, but I was also unable to find the proper person to credit it to. I first heard it from Jim Wallis of Sojourners, but a quick internet search will show other potential originators, as well. My thanks to the mystery wordsmith for a powerful and truthful phrase.

122 This is especially true in regards to the complex, imaginative work the majority of us do, and it turns out that money can actually be de-motivational in these situations. For more on this, read Dan Pink's book *Drive*.

123 Thanks to John Maxwell for this example. You can find it in his book *How Successful People Think*. P.S. This is definitely not a story from my own golfing. Trust me.

124 Of course, the best generals also listen to their soldiers and the best soldiers also think for themselves. Nothing is this black and white in real life, but hopefully the metaphor was somewhat insightful. Apologies for the over*general*ization.

125 This formula is how a person can discover their strongest life; I write more about it on my blog. http://bit.ly/discover-your-strengths

126 I've referenced a ton of these resources in the Endnotes, and I hope you'll check them out. Oh look, you're already there!

127 In the emerging economy, an early casualty will be the "job description" in its current form. The world is reorienting too quickly for this static conceptual dinosaur to survive—already,

they're just a formality. Of course, for them to truly disappear, it will probably require some new governmental structures and rules. The work revolution knows no boundaries.

128 If you doubt the incredible power of motivation, read this short article from Ken Segall on what makes Apple different. http://bit.ly/the-apple-difference

129 I've already mentioned a couple of these unique organizations, including Morning Star and Semco. For another example, check out IDEO. http://bit.ly/ideo-recruiting

130 Read Seth Godin's book *Linchpin* (or follow the link for a free audio download). http://bit.ly/godin-linchpin-session

Silver Thread Publishing is a division of A Silver Thread, LLC.
Colorado 2009 http://asilverthread.com

Publisher has no control over or does not assume any responsibility for author or third-party websites or their content.

Cover by Austyn Elizabeth Ford, Josh Allan Dykstra, & Jason
Walton

Illustrations by Jason Walton
http://waltonportfolio.com

Book design by Austyn Elizabeth Ford
http://austynelizabeth.com

Copy Editing by Nick Kominitsky

Author photograph by Jonathan Kofahl

ISBN 978-0-9858326-1-2
Printed in the United States of America

CPSIA information can be obtained at www.ICGtesting.com
Printed in the USA
LVOW13s2239071013

355762LV00003B/10/P